Bridging the Communication Gap

Bringing Diverse Personalities Together for Successful Engagement

Dr. James J. Haviland

Bridging the Communication Gap

Bringing Diverse Personalities Together for Successful Engagement

Dr. James J. Haviland

To order additional copies of this book, contact:
Xlibris
844-714-8691
www.Xlibris.com
Orders@Xlibris.com
824827

CONTENTS

PREFACE

At the time the first edition of *Bridging the Communication Gap* was released in 2015, I had no idea of the books accuracy in foreshadowing the events that were to take place during the next five years. Both the first edition and this, the second edition, focus on the development and success of the individual reader. There is no focus on the overall social or political agendas that have developed recently within our culture. The focus remains on the sole reader.

The foreshadowing existed by drawing attention to the importance of effective communication and its' apparent decline. The only issue is, I underestimated the magnitude of decline and polarization of opinions that would occur as it relates to communication during this past one-half of a decade. Communication didn't become more difficult, it ceased. Perhaps I should have taken notice of comedian Martin Lawrence's warning in 1992, "Talk to the hand," and realized it was a precursor of what was to come. It was, and is, worse than I had imagined it would be. So, I congratulate myself on my ability to foreshadow. However, we now face a far greater problem as it relates to effective communication. The polarization of opinions, in conjunction with the depersonalization of society due to the pandemic, have created the ingredients for a perfect storm. What form will that storm take?

I introduce the storm-analogy in the realm of communications because there are so many similarities between storms and poor communication. Both have warning signs that are frequently ignored, often with harsh consequences. Prior to a storm, the sky has a greenish tint, wall clouds develop and heavy hail slices through the atmosphere. In communication, it may ignite around arguing over the crowd size at an event. Storms vary in size from hailstorms to typhoons churning at 190 MPH. In communication, the storm may range from silly nick-names to unceremonious dismissals. Both have a considerable span of destruction as an end result to individual reputations and property.

Both storms and breakdowns in communications, require specific circumstances to take place in order to become deadly. In a storm, it requires certain atmospheric moisture, lift and instability. In breakdowns in communication, it requires a culture of self-obsessed, narcissistic individuals influenced by fear and manipulation.

I yield to the power and influence of these variables that exist within our society and I will make no attempt to defend or refute their existence. It is, what it is. Nor is this going to evolve into a treatise on political parties and their respective positions. I'll leave that up to the political pundits, of which there are plenty. Long ago, I declared my independent status until they take public money out of elections and impose term limits. I will stay focused on the individual, without party affiliation and steps they may take to ensure their personal success.

My focus will be on the reader the future generations to come and how they may be touched by the insights gained by the reader. Do I believe the current generation is beyond hope, not beyond, but certainly requiring a significant amount of time in the shop through very little fault of their own I might ad. We are all a product of our times.

This labor of love began a little more than twenty years ago. I was the president of a small college in northern Minnesota and taking advantage of a perk in a system that allows a sabbatical leave of absence for those who qualify. I happened to be one of the fortunate ones. My graduate degrees were in education leadership and business administration. Therefore, I submitted a proposal to study leadership at both the educational and corporate levels. Specifically, leadership traits that defined and contributed to the overall success of a leader both positionally, and ultimately, in salary and/or prestige.

After my sabbatical leave was approved, there was a supervisory position change and the individual who had previously approved of my proposal had been replaced. The new administrator required there be tangible evidence of the efforts put forth during a sabbatical leave. My first book, *This Book Is No Joke!* is the compilation of these efforts.

Reflecting on these efforts, I discovered the number one trait of a successful leader, as well as the number one trait desired in a spouse, was the same; a sense of humor. Not to be confused with jokes or comedy, a true sense of humor is a disposition. The origin of this disposition is found in its name dating back centuries. According to Wilfred Funk, the author of *Word Origins and Their Romantic Stories,* we borrowed the term humor from the Latin, and in the mother language humor meant a liquid. The mixture (Latin: mixture=tempermentum) of bodily fluids would be an indication of one's health i.e. a humorous disposition.

At the risk of infringing on the content of Section V of this manuscript, and Chapter III of the first book, I went on to identify the function of humor in communication, and the role it plays in diffusing conflict with countless examples from master communicators throughout history. Examples were cited from captains of industry, leading political figures, world leaders and quotes from scripture in order to illustrate the significance of humor in communication.

The question of where humor comes from, what happens to it, and how one can regain it was addressed. In addition, research was conducted demonstrating that most people have an inflated sense of their own humor, evidenced by their subordinate evaluations. And rarely, will one admit to an absence of a sense of humor. A sense of humor is viewed as critical to our self-esteem and wellbeing.

The research findings compiled in book form (This Book Is No Joke!) were sufficient to justify a year's absence from campus. The presentation of the research results at the International Platform Association convention in Washington D.C. proved to be award winning.

Prior to my academic experience, I owned my own business in

Australia and upon returning to the states worked as a probation counselor for the prosecutor's office in Kalamazoo, Michigan. I also began teaching theories of juvenile delinquency at a local community college and other courses in the field of criminal justice. I then accepted a faculty position with the department of criminal justice at Northern Michigan University (NMU) in Marquette, Michigan. While at NMU I began a criminal justice association that exposed students to casino security techniques in Las Vegas, Nevada in anticipation that native Americans were going to seek approval for casinos on reservation properties throughout the United States.

I continued my personal educational efforts simultaneously with my academic appointment with Northern Michigan University. I completed my doctorate (Ed.D.) in education leadership at Western Michigan University in Kalamazoo, Michigan. This effort included a sabbatical leave to The University of Las Vegas, Nevada (UNLV) to study the interpretation of Rorschach personality test. I also completed an internship with the homicide bureau in Detroit, Michigan. My doctorial dissertation was completed while assigned to the parole board of Michigan State. It was a study examining the rate of recidivism of inmates completing college associate degrees while incarcerated. Recidivism rates of this cohort were compared to released inmates who did not acquire a degree while incarcerated. This involved the cooperation of Jackson State Prison in Jackson, Michigan, which at the time, housed 6,000 inmates.

I made an abrupt jump from the academic world in Michigan due to an unanticipated opportunity and became the CEO of a professional medical billing service in Presque Isle, Maine. I was subsequently promoted to the position of CEO of the medical foundation sponsoring the billing service.

I soon realized I missed the research and teaching component of higher education and accepted an administrative appointment (Vice Provost) at Northland Community College in northern Minnesota. I was promoted to Provost and then President of the college. I completed a master's in business administration (MBA) at St. Thomas University in St. Paul, Minnesota and subsequently, accepted the position of Senior Fellow for Academic Affairs for the thirty-four colleges in the Minnesota State System. This required me to relocate to St. Paul, Minnesota. In this position I coordinated a leadership program sponsored by the Kellogg Foundation that gained national recognition.

My next career move involved a jump from the academic world to the corporate world. I assumed the position as senior consultant for a sales training organization, Corporate Visions Inc. (CVI) located in Lake Tahoe, Nevada. This required international travel and training resulting in just under two million frequent flyer miles, equivalent to eighty-three trips around the world. I held this position for over a decade. Following this appointment, I became an independent consultant specializing in the area of corporate engagement.

I offer this mini-review of my work experience to convey an overview of my background demonstrating a variety of work environments not only in the United States, but worldwide. I have always been fascinated with what makes certain individuals so much more successful than others. Fortunately, I have had the opportunity in both educational and work environments to pursue the answer to that question. Ironically, I am equally intrigued with the opposite end of the social spectrum, and that is, what makes other people so vulnerable and prone to actions that will nearly guarantee that life will be a series of bad decisions? My education and experience in the field of criminal justice allowed me to gather firsthand knowledge of those volitions or choices that people make that will continue to make them prisoners of yesterdays' decisions.

To the individual experiencing the freedom of society, the concept of prison is a formidable thought. However, research indicates, some inmates become so adaptable they prefer incarceration to the freedom afforded to a law-abiding citizen. "Three snacks and a rack," is an expression of betterment among inmates working for eighteen cents an hour in the laundry room in exchange for free meals, accommodations, vision, dental and health insurance. Throw in some free concerts and cable television, and it's not too shabby of an existence. The only thing missing is some silence every now and then.

Ironically, a considerable number of citizens in free society are unaware they are falling victim to the same influences. By constantly becoming recipients of benefits that are unearned they also are forming psychological dependencies and life on the "outside" becomes a form of "self-imprisonment." This is why the importance of "self-esteem" and its reliance on positive critical decisions and behaviors are emphasized so heavily in this publication. The "On My Way" project in the epilogue focuses on the importance and development of self-esteem in children.

I feel privileged to have the opportunity to share these findings with the reader. With all the diverse cultures, personalities, and political differences along the spectrum of life, one issue remains critical as to which extreme is realized; one's ability to communicate effectively.

When I first addressed the problem back in 2001, I approached it from a positive posture seeking to identify the most desirable trait in effective communication. I now realize, along with the rest of the world, there is a far greater problem than poor communication and that is, no communication. In the first edition of *Bridging the Communication Gap*, released in 2015, I addressed what I had experienced around the world as proven communication techniques, in addition to the most desirable trait, i.e. sense of humor. These techniques are included in this the second edition, and include; critical choices, emotional tones, change avoidance, the influence of technology, and the concept of 'FLOW'.

The first Edition of Bridging the Communication Gap released in 2015, foreshadowed the events that were about to take place. It's not essential to pinpoint precisely when our national disposition began to change from a nation of one, to a nation of self-obsessed individuals. There are a variety of publications that address this social phenomenon, notably; *The Narcissism Epidemic by Twenge & Campbell,* with a cover tag line, "Chronicles the obsession that many Americans have with, well themselves…thinking themselves entitled to things they haven't earned." Also notable; *Selfie, How We Became So Self-Obsessed and What It's Doing to Us by Will Storr.*

Most people are quick to acknowledge that narcissism, an inflated view of the self, is ubiquitous. For those in their teens and younger this is not a new phenomenon. They have entered this world with this dynamic of heighted individualism on full display. It's interesting to note in an audience with a wide range of ages, the youngest have difficulty recognizing, identifying, or acknowledging a cultural shift emphasizing self has occurred. However, the individuals more advanced in age are unanimous in their recognition that such a cultural movement has taken place.

If is very difficult to precisely pinpoint when a cultural shift takes place. It may be a defining moment like the Woodstock concert (8/15-18/1969) that suggest precision dating, or the introduction of the cellphone ('80) or smartphone ('02). For most cultural shifts the timing is vague.

I recently had a discussion with a colleague and suggested it was challenging for any adult over forty to perceive one as intelligent who sprinkles the acronym for "For Unlawful Carnal Knowledge" (more commonly referred to as the F-bomb) throughout their speech. He was amazed that middle-aged people would be offended by the usage of that word. Most people under forty years of age have grown up with the common use of this word. The movie Scarface ('83) drops 208 F-bombs, and Colors ('88) drops 157. If one is a member of the generation where the cultural change takes place it is barely noticeable.

"I first became aware of it one day on the subway," is offered by a conferee. "A young man stepped on the subway holding this huge box on his shoulder blasting out what I assumed to be music that was almost deafening to the rest of the passengers. My fellow passengers quickly made eye-exchanges, as if to convey disbelief of the audacious of his behavior. To this day I wonder, what made him believe that his individual needs were so superior to the rest of us?"

Other attendees were quick to offer their individual epiphanies as to when they realized there had been an alteration to the cultural norms. For one it was when she saw a bumper sticker, "I Love Me." For another, it was when she read about a woman who changed her 2-year-old son's name from Kevin to Kelvin to match the misspelled tattoo of his name on her arm. Another shared the accounting of a 31-year-old Florida woman who sent more than 65,000 text messages to a man with whom she had just one date. One of my favorites is advice offered by an Australian "sexuality educator" that parents should ask their baby's permission before changing diapers. She goes on to explain, "just by asking the parents are letting that child know that their response matters." I now realize my mom owes me some apologies!

One of my "aha" moments that something in the culture had changed was during the late seventies. It was in the movie, *Saturday Night Fever* (1977), and John Travolta was painstaking grooming his hair and fastidiously tucking his silk shirt in preparation for his night on the town. Later, watching his "all about me" entrance to the discotheque and his subsequent line-dance that mesmerized the standing-room only audience, it occurred to me what was missing in his preparation for the event. What was different from what I would experience, was any thought or involvement of his girl or date for the evening. It was as if she didn't exist in order for him to have this fulfilling evening.

Another reflection for me that times were changing was the celebrity that Joe Namath received during his football career with Alabama and later with the New York Jets. His white fur coat gleaned as much attention as the game and his famously quoted line, "I can't wait for tomorrow, because I get better looking every day," lives on. And times have changed.

My contribution to this psychological development was a workshop entitled; *Therapy on a Stick*. The primary premise of this seminar is the belief that society has created a toxic environment for our youth by perpetuating an illusion "to strive for social perfectionism." The unfortunate part is the definition of perfection is defined by social media and constantly changing. This uncertainty creates a variety of repercussions ranging from anxiety, depression, addiction, body image distortion, isolation and unfortunately, more than 45,000 suicides annually. Each of these deaths have their own circumstances. However, the lack of support and communication with stable support systems that were readily available in the past, including friends, neighbors, community organizations and relatives living nearby, now resides, "in-the-cloud." The pillars of support that were once readily available for communication remain available, however only at their convenience.

Is this period of self-obsession only temporary? One may hope so. However, it has proven to be resilient as it approaches its fiftieth-anniversary, with no sign of letting up thanks to social media.

The trouble with life is, you are halfway through before you realize it is one of those 'do-it-yourself' deals.
-Unleash Your Greatness (Olson & Strand)

INTRODUCTION

I sincerely believe to be in the presence of one communicating effectively is comparable to listening to a beautiful piece of music, watching a priceless work of art unfold on a canvas, watching an artisan complete a clay molding or a glass blower completing his work of art with a precise flick of the wrist. To watch one flow from pleasant conversation with the neighbor, to light exchanges with the bag boy at the grocery store, to colleagues at work, with supervisors and subordinates, to loved ones at home is nothing short of watching a royal ballet being performed at center stage. It is beauty to behold.

This ability to communicate like a master craftsman does not come naturally. It takes years of varied experiences and a multitude of situations to learn the craft. It requires the flexibility of a journeyman and the strength of a gladiator to hold firm and defend a position you know is right. It requires the empathy of a nun and the magic of a firefly to abruptly change luminescence when another person enters the room.

Unfortunately, if one were forced to reveal the name of one who possessed this quality to communicate effectively, one most likely would reach for the history books and produce one of few that come to mind: Gandhi, Thoreau, or possibly Christ. Dale Carnegie ran into this problem nearly one hundred years ago when the University of Chicago and the United Y.M.C.A. Schools conducted a survey to determine what adults want to study. The survey revealed that health is the prime interest of adults, and their second interest is people: how to understand and get along with people, how to make people like you, and how to win others to your way of thinking.

A leading capitalist at the time, John D. Rockefeller echoed the same by stating, "The ability to deal with people is as purchasable a commodity as sugar or coffee. And I will pay more for that ability than for any other under the sun."

At this time the search was on to find the textbook that would accompany the critical course. According to Dale Carnegie, the end result was the confession, "I know what those adults want. But the book they need has never been written." Carnegie began the class, starting with a set of rules printed on a card no larger than a postcard. The next season they printed a larger card, then a leaflet, than a series of booklets, and after fifteen years of experiment and research came the book, *How to Win Friends & Influence People*. Eighty years later; the concern remains and the resources are still lacking.

Bridging the Communication Gap attempts to fill in some of the potholes that have accumulated during those eighty years while recognizing some of the aspirations of the current reader. For openers, the earlier concerns discovered by the Y.M.C.A. are as relevant today as they were eighty years ago. Many would argue the communication, or lack thereof, problem has become worse, and there are several reasons for this. We have lived through an age of tremendous growth including the innovation of the pill, electronics, computers, and the birth of the internet. In addition, we have television, antibiotics, space travel, civil rights, feminism, teenagers, the green revolution, gay rights, high speed trains and cars, and walking on the moon. All are relevant and exciting accomplishments, and discussions relating to effective communication pale alongside these advancements.

Many of the technological advancements have impinged on our ability to communicate, and they are more engaging than just "talking." This common concurrence makes it acceptable for all members of the family to indulge in modern media while out to dinner. In the old days, it might just be dad who would disengage and read the paper while others conversed. The limitation on the number of characters in addition to the expectation of an immediate response has limited our patience and our attention span to that of a hummingbird. To suggest a "family discussion" over any given issue is tantamount to a suicide pact.

I notice the latest communication technique that seems to be in vogue is to just increase your volume if you want your opinion known and/or to talk over the person who is offering an opposing view. This technique seems to be gaining momentum on a daily basis.

I don't begrudge any of the advances, just the acknowledgement that referencing back to a problem (communication) that has existed well over one hundred years is not nearly as interesting as talking about the latest release from Apple. Which is more appealing, talking about the new 50" flat screen to be placed on the den wall or the septic tank system that must be replaced? No doubt the flat screen will be up, and the septic will continue to fester.

In any event, this book is written with the contemporary reader in mind. It spares the reader of undue research by providing an ample listing of resources in the back of the book. It has one very clear and simple purpose, and that is to allow the reader to challenge the author regarding the techniques suggested. Each of the concepts is presented with the intent that it will make the reader more aware and at the same time more assertive in becoming an effective communicator. It is anticipated and expected that the reader will apply the concept immediately.

The book deals with communication, more specifically, with the lack thereof in contemporary society. More importantly, it addresses how an individual may communicate more effectively by merging a few concepts, presented in a simplistic fashion without undue time and resources committed to theoretical explanations and academic arguments. In short, these techniques work and this is why.

The book begins with an overview of the role of engagement in the contemporary workplace. I focus on this because I believe the word "engagement" is the "twenty-first century in-word" in the business lexicon. Like the word "motivation," I believe the term "engagement" will have an active shelf-life that approaches 100 years. It will be used indiscriminately by consultants like me to justify outrageous fees, and reserve the right to define it as the situation requires. According to Maylett and Warner, organizations currently spend about $720 million a year in the United States alone on programs intended to increase employee engagement. And that figure is expected to double.

This section will focus on the key drivers as well as the benefits of engagement to an organization. It will emphasize the role of the supervisor as it relates to engagement and how to communicate effectively in order to enhance engagement. The key roadblocks to engagement will be introduced, and the most popular escape routes that make the exchange of information more difficult will be revealed.

In Section II, we will examine the role of communication as it relates to the ability to develop relationships and the perceived value of this ability as it relates to success and income in the real world. It answers the question, "How can one person be so much more valuable than another to an organization?"

In Section III, I begin to drift down the path of self-indulgence. As a lifelong educator in the classroom or the boardroom, as well as a former college president, I have always been fascinated by the lack of communication that takes place within the "ivory tower" of higher education. This section of reflection will clarify to the reader why it is the faculty members don't like the students, the administration, or the institution. Yes, it has to do with communication. However, I felt compelled to include this chapter, since the book is written from the perspective of a college classroom. This setting was ideal to communicate the relevant concerns of bridging the communication gap in a creative nonfiction format.

Section IV takes us down another slippery slope as we examine the critical traits of leadership in an attempt to isolate the most critical trait of all. Section V identifies this critical trait and expands its origins, its demise, and the necessary steps to take to revive it.

In Section VI, we examine the steps necessary to achieve high self-esteem and in Section VII the choices one must make on a daily and even an hourly bases to assure a high level of self-esteem.

Assuming people are able to exercise the appropriate choices in order to achieve high self-esteem, how do they recognize and choose the people of a like quality in order to assure effective communication takes place? This becomes the focus of Section VIII.

Once people reach this pinnacle of achievement, exercising full and effective communication to assure personal and professional success, how do they continue to be challenged? This question becomes the focus of Section IX.

Given the blueprint of success in Sections I through IX, why would anyone refuse to become fully engaged in becoming all they can be? Enter Section X, which examines why it is that people refuse to make the necessary changes in lifestyle in order to become fully actualized.

Section XI provides an isolated example of the power of resistance that exist within all of us to withstand the influence of outside forces and opinions to modify an established behavior, even if it is for our own betterment.

The final section, Section XII, concludes by drawing the reader's attention to the influence that technology has had on communication over the past fifty years. In summary, we have grown lazy in our efforts to innovate new technologies since our roller coaster ride in the "Golden Quarter" (1945 to 1971). We have improved our technologies, but for the most part they are not "new" or "innovative" technologies. But nowhere is our laziness more apparent than our inability to communicate with one another. We have been lulled to sleep in the most important aspect of our lives as we attempt to relate to those we work with, live next to, and love the most.

SECTION I

Engagement

"*Why* is it that we can get along with virtually any human being we come in contact with, with the exception of our immediate supervisor?" It can be a complete stranger; it can be someone who has inadvertently called the wrong number, or someone we have been matched with through a number of dating services. All of these adventitious meetings will be more celebrated than the daily exchange we have with our supervisor.

More challenging may be an acceptable explanation as to why, immediately following our promotion, do we immediately become the lead leper in the colony? So begins the onslaught of questions accompanying a new set of graduate students and a new semester. A new semester that will review management theory and leadership proposals that have survived the scrutiny of time and will remain for decades to come. Let us begin with a contemporary term that has captured the imagination of many in the field of leadership theory: engagement.

One of the great chasms that exists in communication is the gap between employer and employee. More specifically, the gap between supervisor and employee is a critical concern that carries considerable impact if not resolved. This dynamic is frequently the deciding factor determining if one continues to pursue a career in a specific field or elects to move on to other challenges and opportunities. This gap has a huge influence on the home environment as a significant member of the household carries home a disposition strongly influenced by the communication or lack thereof that takes place between two employees on any given day. It is the plague that circulates among employees in the work environment but remains unmentioned until "disengagement" mentally or physically takes place.

Few terms in recent years have captured the imagination of the business community like the term, "engagement." Not since Abraham Maslow introduced his theory of Motivation Hierarchy in 1954 in his book, *Motivation and Personality*, have we embraced a concept so willingly and completely. Both engagement and motivation have similar appeal. They make very abstract concepts visually appealing to an intuitive mind. Therein lies their power and popularity.

My introduction to Maslow dates back to psychology classes in high school and college. The theory simply states that man has certain basic needs: food, water, and shelter to survive. These needs are expressed at the base of an imaginary pyramid and once these needs are satisfied, an individual is motivated to seek the next higher level needs. This upward progression continues as long as the lower needs are met and ultimately culminates at the highest level, or in Maslow's terms, a self-actualized individual.

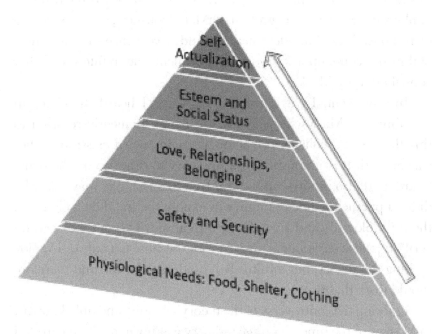

Maslow's Hierarchy of Needs

In spite of the popularity of Maslow's theory, I vividly recall one professor throwing Maslow under the bus by quoting a work which if memory serves me right was entitled; *Maslow Revisited*. According to this professor, Maslow's work reflected the results of a very small and inadequate sampling of individuals, and within that sampling there are few if any significant findings to indicate that individuals would progress up this hierarchy of needs once the lower needs were met and little evidence to indicate that all people desire these unique or specific needs. This argument would suggest there are many people who are quite content to stay at the lower levels of the pyramid, opposed to pursuing higher aspirations.

Recently, David Zweig has identified another very prominent grouping of workers who fail to conform to Maslow's hierarchy of progression. Zweig refers to these individuals and collectively as "Invisibles" in his recent book entitled *Invisibles: The Power of Anonymous Work in an Age of Relentless Self-Promotion (2014)*. According to Zweig, these hidden professionals (Invisibles) embody three traits: 1) Ambivalence toward recognition, 2) Meticulousness, and 3) Savoring of responsibility. The identification and acceptance of this cohort within the contemporary work environment may refute the earlier contribution by Maslow.

In any event, I was bummed out when I heard the criticism pertaining to Maslow's work because I had frequently resorted to this theory as a college instructor on nights when classroom filler was needed. It is simplistic in nature, easy to draw up on the white board, and also intuitive in nature. In retrospect, one may ask, why didn't I pursue the line of inquiry to expose the fraudulent claims of the psychologist? And I would have to admit, I wasn't too keen on verifying the accusations against Maslow because not only did I enjoy reciting the theory, but intuitively it made good sense and therefore should work that way.

Ignoring the controversy of the theory's validity and unbeknownst to Maslow at the time, a cottage industry was born, revolving around the word "motivation." Overnight, theories of motivation sprang to life. Rats became a desired commodity, speaker bureaus were a buzz, and workshop venues were at a premium. A new breed of consultant reared its ugly head that continues to this day, the motivational speaker.

In addition to the widespread use of the term motivation, another twenty-first century term that has gained wide acceptance in the lexicon of the businessman's vocabulary is the term "engagement."

According to *Talent Management* magazine (August 2014), many cite the arrival of the term "engagement," and insertion into the management lexicon with a 1999 *Institute for Employment Studies* article, which examined the link between frontline worker happiness and customer satisfaction in the service industry.

Employee Engagement is defined as "the emotional commitment to the organization and its goals." In the past, an engaged employee would be referred to as one willing to go that extra mile for the team. Researchers in the field frequently note that the use of "we"' opposed to "me" is one of the speech patterns of the truly engaged employee. Similar to motivation, engagement has such a positive and desirable overtone and it is hard to imagine one not supportive of its suggested outcomes. In clarifying the definition, the engaged employee is further recognized for one's behaviors in discretionary situations. The difficulty of defining what is and is not a discretionary effort is more of a challenge. If people stoop to pick up trash that has been carelessly discarded in the parking lot, are they doing so out of love and commitment to the company, or are they merely environmentally self-conscious?

The attraction to engagement is the same as the attraction to motivation. What's not to like? They both reek of optimism and future positive outcomes. Both have a deterministic quality that is hard not to support and comfortably project anticipated outcomes supported by research in their respective fields.

The characteristics or environmental traits that contribute or influence an environment supporting an atmosphere conducive to engagement are referred to as drivers. These drivers will vary in degree of emphasis and frequency of delivery but are recognized to be the distinguishing quality or characteristics of engagement.

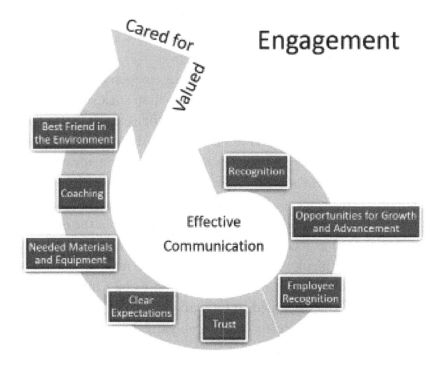

Drivers to Engagement

The major drivers of engagement are effective communication, continuous employee recognition, opportunities for employee growth and advancement, and an overall atmosphere of trust amongst employees as well as between employees and management.

Secondary drivers to engagement are clearly defined expectations of the employee, availability of materials and equipment needed to meet the established expectations, and knowledgeable coaching when needed. Engaged employees must sense that their opinions are not only heard but valued by the administrative team. Employees respond favorably when they feel cared about and when their progress is noted by their supervisor or management team. Current research also suggest engaged employees perform better when they have a significant or best friend working in the same environment.

To be engaged and emotionally committed to an organization

and its goals is to anticipate a variety of positive results for the organization including greater productivity, higher profits, increased worker and customer satisfaction, customer loyalty and retention, lower rates of absenteeism and turnover, fewer quality defects and safety violations, and a considerable degree of customer loyalty. The organization will also benefit from lower rates of turnover, product shrinkage (theft), quality defects, and work place accidents. Once again, what's not to like? Everybody wins!

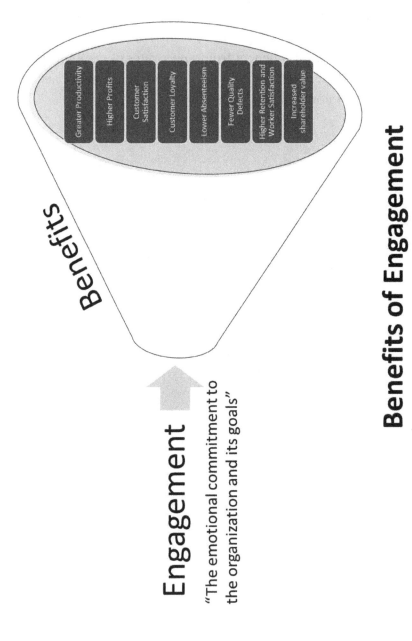

Benefits

Greater Productivity

Higher Profits

Customer Satisfaction

Customer Loyalty

Lower Absenteeism

Fewer Quality Defects

Higher Retention and Worker Satisfaction

Increased shareholder value

Engagement

"The emotional commitment to the organization and its goals"

Benefits of Engagement

Research supporting the above claims is readily available and abundant. Kevin Kruse's book, *Employee Engagement 2.0 (2012)*, is an excellent resource containing 28 research findings demonstrating a correlation between employee engagement and the desired outcomes mentioned above. For backup, I always carry his earlier work co-authored with Rudy Karsan, *How To Increase Performance and Profits Through Full Engagement (2011)*. This book is also an excellent resource based on research from Kenexa, a company that conducts employee engagement and opinion surveys for more than 10 million workers in over 150 countries each year. I figured that was an adequate sampling; however, if truth be known, I have rarely been questioned regarding the legitimacy of the claims made by experts in the field of engagement. I suspect the reason for that is the concept is so appealing intuitively. What manager or owner would state that it wasn't of interest or importance to them to increase productivity, profits, etc.?

As a consultant in the field of employee engagement, I have come to some conclusions relating to the overall process of evaluating current rates of engagement as well as introducing steps to improve future levels of engagement. The primary method for determining current rates of engagement is the administration of a survey, electronic or paper/pencil, and conducted by a member of the human resources department.

I would strongly advise against utilizing in-house personnel or utilizing an electronic survey instrument for a couple of reasons. It has been my experience that the most prevalent factor leading to disengagement is a breakdown of communication within the organization. Surrounding this breakdown in communication is frequently an atmosphere of distrust. Now which came first, the breakdown in communication or the distrust, can become a chicken and egg discussion, but is somewhat irrelevant. At this point, they feed off one another, and any attempt to gather pertinent data from individuals or technology that may be traceable within the organization is met with a great deal of skepticism at best. Nevertheless, any results or future efforts to enhance engagement will be met with resistance given the questionable origin and reliability of the data. Save yourself the trouble; go outside the organization for data collection.

Most of the literature relating to engagement will suggest an organization is better off not introducing initial engagement surveys or efforts relating to engagement if there is no intent to follow up on the findings that result. I disagree with this. I have found there to be tremendous value in hiring outside expertise in the field to come in to an organization and simultaneously conduct an employee interview while administering the survey instrument. The interview may be very broad in nature, inquiring about what brought an employee to the organization, how they have progressed, what challenges they have encountered and what suggestions and/or recommendations they may have to make the work environment more pleasant and productive.

The opportunity to merely express their concerns and be heard is of tremendous value to the employee. And to keep it in perspective, the truth of the matter is employee expectations are rather modest with respect to any outcomes or expectations that may materialize as a result of their engagement interview. However, that doesn't negate the benefits to be derived from the experience. For the most part, employees have worked for years victims of policies dictated from above. To be heard by an independent party is perceived to be a giant step forward for most employees.

I recently interviewed more than 1,500 employees from a very successful company in a somewhat isolated area representing a population of 8,600 residents. I discovered what I consider to be another significant driver of engagement that others involved in engagement theory have not introduced, and that is the impact of geographic isolation as it relates to engagement.

Assume that an organization is located in a very remote and isolated area and has a very competitive salary and a Cadillac of a benefits package. The conversation relating to alternative employment opportunities, if desired, takes on a completely different tone. If one desires to change employment for any particular reason, it becomes a much greater issue than merely adjusting one's commute to a different location. If one wants to match both salary and benefits, it means physical relocating and all that accompanies that decision.

Geographical isolation appears to encourage engagement or the emotional commitment to the organization because the loss of employment would be so devastating to the lifestyle established. Ironically, this isolation may even be detrimental to some of the other key drivers of engagement like communication and trust. One may be hesitant to confide in a fellow worker or express discontentment of any manner, in fear of personality conflicts in the future, or reprisal, possibly in the form of dismissal. In short, when there is little, if any, comparable competition in the area, employees may experience a great deal of fear or mistrust, nevertheless rating the organization relatively high on factors relating to engagement (work satisfaction, alternative job searching, recommending the current employer).

For most employees, an engagement event will be the first and last time someone has sincerely asked for their input regarding the workplace. And this observation includes annual reviews conducted by supervisors, etc., bearing in mind the earlier observation that most bureaucracies exist in an atmosphere girdled in mistrust and poor communication, not to mention the in-house personnel conducting the interview may easily be the major bone of contention.

For those employees who are intimidated by the one-on-one interview seeking their input for suggestions and new ideas, I would recommend having a copy of Sam Parker's book, *212 the Extra Degree*, on hand. This compact little handbook illustrates the reality that heating water to 211 degrees produces very hot water, but adding just one more degree of heat takes it to 212 degrees and it boils, producing the steam energy sufficient to power a locomotive. What appears to be a small, tiny increment of change may trigger major changes having lasting impact on an organization.

For example, I recently witnessed the impact that introducing a shuttle for employees to their vehicles had on an organization located in northern Minnesota, granted that walk to the car following the night shift may hover in the sub-zero range as the wind whips across the plains in northern Minnesota. It's gestures like this that contribute to employees feeling "safe," the desirable state employees seek that James Hunter refers to in his book, *The Servant*. This "I've got your back" feeling from the management team is what employees long for and is certainly a characteristic of an engaged work environment. Employees feel valued in such an atmosphere.

With regard to the observation that one would be better off doing nothing than asking for input with no follow through, most employees have such low expectations that anything will ever result from their input, it is very hard to disappoint them by a limited response. Unfortunately, the bar is set very low in most instances, and employees are grateful just for the opportunity to express their concerns.

I frequently advise companies that are aware of high levels of disengagement (usually evident by high turnover) but may not have the funds or are unwilling to conduct the initial survey to first determine the specific areas where drivers are deficient to invest in training their supervisors. The relationship between the employee and their immediate supervisor is the primary key to high levels of engagement. If this relationship is not solid, there will continue to be a heavy, if not terminal effect on the organization. This applies to all levels of supervision within the organization.

The immediate question from the administration is in what areas should the training for the supervisors be directed? I pause to reflect on how most supervisors obtained their positions and sadly reflect on the dark side of that mobility. Most supervisors obtain their current positions by excelling in the task consistent with their previous position. Success and competence in performance yields promotion, frequently to supervisor. Unfortunately, the down side of this popular mobility phenomenon was exposed nearly fifty years ago by a Canadian academic, Laurence J. Peter in his best seller, *The Peter Principle (1969)*.

The Peter Principle states that managers rise to their level of incompetence. They are continuously promoted until they fail to do well in their current job. The final promotion is from a level of competence to a level of incompetence. In short, people are promoted to a level of incompetence, and this is when the promotions cease. This promotion is unfortunate for those whom the newly promoted will now supervise.

The second most popular avenue to a supervisory role or upper management position is to be an individual who interviews well. Again, this ability to interview well is no certainty that one will perform well, just recognition that they interview well. In any event, when the interview is the primary or sole criteria for promotion, there shouldn't be a great deal of surprise from the administration when there is a breakdown in communication between employee and supervisor resulting in disengagement or lack of emotional commitment to the organization. Frequently, the reward for doing a mechanical or technical job well is to be promoted to a position that requires an entirely new set of skills, including interpersonal skills, with minimal or limited training. This lack of skills and preparation in interpersonal relations frequently results in a defensive demeanor from the newly appointed supervisor who is fearful of being exposed.

In response to the training question, what would you suggest we do to bring our supervisors up to speed? At the risk of dating myself, I would quickly suggest Dale Carnegie's, *How to Win Friends and Influence People* book and course. Too often I see organizations clamoring for the latest management theory or technique in order to bring the skills of their management team up to date. What's needed has stood the test of time, given the predictability of people, and their desire to feel important and appreciated. These are basic, basic skills, but unfortunately never taught and frequently overlooked. Check out Carnegie's table of contents:

- Give honest, sincere appreciation;
- Arouse in the other person an eager want;
- The only way to get the best of an argument is to avoid it;
- Show respect for the other person's opinions. Never say, "You're Wrong."
- Ask questions instead of giving direct orders;

- Let the other person save face.

This is just a sampling of the interpersonal skills to which most supervisors have had limited exposure. All efforts directed toward the refinement of these interpersonal skills are a tremendous step toward closing the communication gap that exists.

Eventually, as directors of HR and concerned parties extend efforts to identify or recognize what it is within their organizations that is causing low morale, high turnover, and a plethora of other undesirable outcomes, they will conclude the culprit to be "poor communication." In an effort to save countless hours of internal examination, I would like to offer a quick fix based on decades of experience in the field. Enemy number one to ineffective communication will most likely be incomplete information.

Perhaps I should be more explicit. Information is incomplete when it does not specifically relate to the needs, wants, and desires of the employee. Employees simply want to know, how can you and/ or your solution help me? Period! They are not concerned about the resources you have access to, your success within the industry, or your market share. When new policies, rules, and regulations are introduced, employees would like a courtesy reminder of what is currently being done, know **why** a change has been initiated, **how** it will be implemented, and lastly, **how it will affect them personally.** They simply want to know how your solution will make it a better world for them. Anything else is propaganda.

The diagram below illustrates how new policies are typically introduced, followed by an illustration of the way employees prefer to receive new information. If they choose to avoid the more detailed explanation, they can be assured of an avalanche of water-cooler discussion attempting to decipher who, how, and why the change was introduced. These discussion points are inevitable, and until they are resolved in the mind of the employee, there will be degrees of resistance and sabotage regarding the change.

Policy Change Example

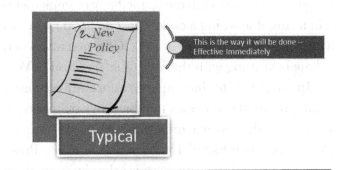

Effective Communication

What if there was an established procedure that every new policy, rule, and regulation introduced contained these four elements of explanation: present procedure, need for change, how it will work and lastly how it would affect the employee? This is the type of communication that employees seek. This is how employees begin to feel valued, and this type of communication instills commitment, support, loyalty, and involvement that contributes to the overall atmosphere of trust, a fundamental cornerstone to engagement. This closes the communication gap between supervisor and employee drastically.

I'm sure some would argue that employees are informed on a "need to know bases," and this approach will slow down the communication process. I think initially this is true; however, in the end, the long range benefits outweigh the immediacy of implementation. Think of it in terms of teaching a child. "Just do it!" may influence immediate action, but it will be temporary, challenged and a constant source of debate beginning with the inevitable question of Why? Why? Why?

In addition to incomplete information contributing to the communication gap, enemy number two would be not communicating within the desired learning channel of the employee. According to research conducted by Neuro Linguistic Programing (NLP) practitioner, it is vital to recognize that individuals have a preferred learning channel when receiving new information. Some desire information in a verbal form, others prefer visual stimulation, and others are more kinesthetic in nature. It is not up to the source or originator of the information to determine which channel is the preferred channel but to assure that all three channels are addressed or activated. No doubt my verbal explanation of Maslow's Hierarchy of Needs was acceptable to the auditory learners, and I'm sure the visual learners appreciated the diagram. To reach the kinesthetic learners who need to be more actively involved in the learning process, I would need to get them more physically active, perhaps asking them to either place a dot on the pyramid to indicate their present stage of development or write specific actions that would indicate their involvement at each level of development. The physical action of writing engages the kinesthetic mind.

In order to make communication relevant to the receivers, they must be able to clearly identify why the suggested change is taking place, how it will occur, how it affects them, and ideally presented in a manner conducive to how they learn best, whether it be visual, auditory, or kinesthetic.

The ability to communicate to a specific learning channel other than one preferred by the individual sending the message can be more challenging than first anticipated. As a visual learner myself, I make it a practice to have clients draw as we begin our interview. I resort to some standby expressions in order to make this happen.

I may ask an engineer (frequently kinesthetic) to "Illustrate to me where you fit into the organization or illustrate where you see the conflict," or "Show me where the bottleneck exists." I will always have some props near in order to convert a visual explanation to a kinesthetic explanation. I never apologize for the request, and if I see any hesitation, I merely request, "I'm a visual learner and in order to better assist you, I need an illustration."

As authority figures continue to choose to be comfortable opposed to effective in their communication, it is inevitable that they will continue to be dysfunctional. This phenomenon, blatantly observed in bureaucracies, introduces enemy number three, the development silos of information. In silos, information becomes the currency and therefore only shared with those individuals or departments that have similar views and goals. Many consider this non-transparent silo environment as not so much a matter of personalities each seeking to be heard but simply a lack of shared direction. The only way to break through these silos, short of cleaning house, is to pursue common goals that require team participation. In most bureaucracies where there is frequently an absence of trust as well as an avoidance of accountability, a positive outcome is difficult at best but not impossible. In the absence of commitment, the communication gap will only become wider.

Silos of Information

Lencioni, has done an admirable job outlining the end result of this sort of turf/information protectiveness in his book, *The 5 Dysfunction of a Team*. He identifies the glaring evidence when a team is dysfunctional by identifying the five major dysfunctions of a team: lack of commitment, fear of conflict, avoidance of accountability, inattention to results, and lack of trust. It has been my professional experience and opinion that it becomes relatively easy to predict which escape route will be exercised by any given authority figure in order to maintain an appearance of cooperation and avoid any hint of not being a team player. Modifying Lencioni's options, meetings take on the atmosphere of attempting to guess which avenue or exit will be taken (see illustration below).

Pick your Escape Route

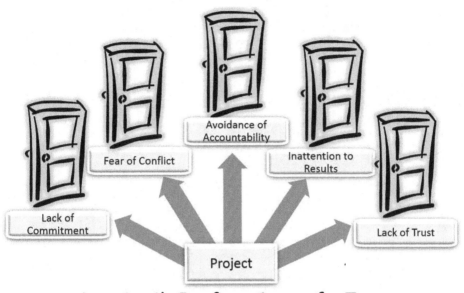

Lencioni's Dysfunctions of a Team

Individual mannerisms, limited contributions, and excuses serve to reveal an individual's favorite escape route rather easily. Lencioni identifies the five doors above as repercussions of a dysfunctional team that become barriers that turn colleagues into competitors. I would suggest that they are also well worn escape routes that stifle the exchange of information and make the communication gap wider still.

The earlier in the process one detects the desired exit route of a team member, the less disappointing it will be as projects lag, delays are prevalent, and results are postponed for no apparent reason. Let us return to the classroom.

SECTION II

Perceived Value

"Dr. Haviland, would you consider an executive's ability to establish a high level of engagement the key to making them worth almost $500.00 an hour?" The class, Emerging Patterns of Leadership, was a graduate class in the public administration program.

"What makes you ask, and why did you pick that hourly rate?" I inquired.

"Well, the most recent edition of Forbes Magazine has released the salaries and compensation of the leading CEO's, and a lot of these guys are making more than $1,000,000 a year."

"Yes, that's probably true, but where does the $500.00 an hour come into play?"

"That was my calculation. I calculated a forty hour work week for fifty-two weeks a year and came up with two thousand and eighty hours of work in a year. I divided the million a year salary by the two thousand and eighty hours worked and came up with over $400.00 an hour, $480.76, to be precise."

"That sounds accurate," I responded, still trying to figure out where this was going and conscious of the fact this discussion had little to do with my lesson plan. Nevertheless, the other members of the class seemed to enjoy the exchange. *"Do you think most CEOs only work a forty hour week?"* I challenged.

"No, I think most would claim they work a lot more, but this doesn't really reflect holidays, a minimum of four weeks for vacation and a boatload of other bennies we all know they get. Think of it, these guys make over one hundred and fifteen dollars when they take a fifteen minute coffee break. It just doesn't seem fair."

This was a moment frozen in time for me. Quite frankly, I don't recall exactly how the exchange between the two of us ended some twenty-five years ago. However, I suspect I said something relating to the dynamics of compensation and leadership in an attempt to lead us back to the syllabus and the lecture I had planned for the evening.

The exchange that evening remains a bench mark, not only due to the emotional trauma I experienced my first night teaching graduate school, but more importantly a deep seated and to some extent unconscious concern that I had harbored for some twenty-five years and would continue to research for the next twenty-five years. How could one person be so much more valuable to an organization than another? And more pointedly, how could I become that person? The mystery lay before me. My quest became to solve the mystery of what constitutes individual financial value or worth to an organization and to discern how this dynamic or trait is transferred to personal relationships. If in fact this trait is transferable to personal relationships, it becomes priceless. This book reflects the journey experienced in solving the mystery. Enjoy the journey. Enjoy the future.

Unbeknownst to my father, he was a significant influence on me and my quest to uncover the dynamics of leadership. From his earlier years as a boyhood farmer in Iowa, he became a door-to-door salesman of pots and pans. I envisage him as an outgoing, gregarious sociable salesman of the Elmer Gantry or Music Man's Professor Howard Hill mold. My father attended Morningside College in Iowa and was the captain of the football team, president of his class, a member of the debate team, and as my mother would attest, *"A striking handsome clothes hound, with the whitest shirts I've ever seen."*

My father went to Creighton Medical School and as the story goes, due to the Depression era times, he was not financially able to continue with his education. As our family began, he became the breadwinner. My earliest memories of him were as a postman and a night bartender, with a sideline of selling pots and pans. I include this historical footnote as a reflection on a man who was extremely competent and proud. Yet due to financial hardships and a growing family, he had to sacrifice his dreams and leave them behind. Not once did I ever hear him resort to the "pity party" of how unfair the world had been to him. When we traveled down memory lane and he reflected on his life, he would admit; *"The biggest mistake I ever made was being too proud to ask others for help when I needed it. I can only imagine how our lives would have been different."*

My father did not lose his ability to enjoy the company of others. I was envious of the way he could attract others to him. One particular insight became instrumental in my quest to discover the mysterious traits of leadership. In my youth, along with my two brothers, we delivered the morning *Detroit Free Press* to the homes and businesses in our town of Drayton Plains, Michigan approximately thirty miles north of Detroit. I would collect payment on Friday evenings when most people were home; however, there was also a hidden agenda for collecting late on Fridays. I delivered to one favorite lounge that was particularly warm and friendly to me, primarily because my father was the bartender.

I would enter in about eight in the evening, saunter up to the bar and request payment for the *Detroit Free Press*. My father would lean over the bar and tell me to take a seat at the little table at the far end of the bar and he would get to me as soon as possible. "In the meantime, would I like a coke as I waited?" This charade would play out week after week. And I loved every minute of it, especially near Christmas when the bar lights would be twinkling, frequently highlighting the sounds from a little combo playing up front, and the hum of conversation would blend with the constant laughter and tinkle of ice cubes against glass. Dad was well known in these parts because he delivered mail and sold pots and pans door-to-door in addition to bartending.

The table would frequently fill with friends as I enjoyed the music, the laughter, and the commotion. The conversation would jump from sports to politics to local events and inevitably, usually about the time we were about to leave, out of the blue one of the customers would yell out, "Say Paul, round me up a set of those three saucepans, will ya?" The pans that Dad peddled during the day were conveniently on display at the back of the bar. "It'll be great as a surprise."

"I'll drop them off Tuesday, and say hi to Carol," Dad would respond. Having experienced this transaction on several occasions, I was forced to make a confession to my dad.

"Dad, I don't get it. I never hear you trying to sell anybody anything. I never hear you talking about pots and pans. Yet several times when we walk out, somebody puts in an order for pots and pans." He let out a big laugh.

"Son, rarely is it about the product. They can get the same set of pans right down the street or one that's lighter weight and cheaper at the hardware."

"So why do they buy from you?" I asked.

"It's all about relationships, Son. It's all about relationships," he grinned. *"I'll explain it when we get home."*

That evening we settled down for hot chocolate at the kitchen table, and he gave me his threadbare copy of Dale Carnegie's *How to Win Friends and Influence People.*

"Son, when you read this, you'll understand what I meant when I said it's not about the product. Next to the Bible, this is the most important book you'll ever read in your life. Far more important than anything I ever read in college."

I have been hooked since that day and remain a lifetime fan of Carnegie. Ironically, Carnegie supplied a discussion point of the graduate class as other members of the class began to contribute.

"Do you think a CEO is that far superior to the rest of us?" A young woman asked. This prompted another student to inquire.

"Are they that smart or technologically savvy?"

It was now more than a quarter of a century since I had read Carnegie for the first time, and yet this was an opportune moment for me to quote one of the studies from the Carnegie Institute of Technology.

According to Carnegie, *"Investigations revealed that even in such technical lines as engineering, about 15 percent of one's financial success is due to one's technical knowledge and about 85 percent is due to skill in human engineering—to personality and the ability to lead people."*

"That's only one study," a skeptical voice from the back of the room shouted.

"No, as I recall, Zig Ziglar quotes the Carnegie study and references three other reputable institutions that replicated the Carnegie study, resulting in the same statistical outcomes." I welcomed this opportunity to sound professorial and to capture a fraction of my investment in higher education which focused exclusively on theories of leadership.

"Dr. Haviland, do you think it's the CEO's personality or the CEO's ability to lead that makes them so valuable?"

"Would it sound like a cop-out if I said I think it's a combination of the two? I believe that some individuals possess a personality trait that enables them to lead more effectively than others. Does that work for you?"

"I don't know. Is it a trait that can be identified with a price tag put on it?" He asked.

"I'm not sure the specific trait has been identified, but some feel that the end result, the ability to lead, carries a price tag. John D. Rockefeller said, 'The ability to deal with people is as purchasable a commodity as sugar or coffee. And I will pay more for that ability, than for any other under the sun.' Pretty strong endorsement, I would say." And this endorsement is certainly consistent with the earlier discussions relating to engagement, Carnegie, and my father.

SECTION III

The Ivory Tower

I was amazed. At this point we hadn't touched on any topic that I had so laboriously outlined for the evening. Nor had I even passed out the course syllabus. My plan was to hand out the syllabus and then very diligently proceed to outline in great detail the requirements of the class pertaining to attendance, grading, etc. I planned to answer any questions they may have had, anticipating there would be none, and then dismiss early to offer them an opportunity for the purchase of texts at the bookstore. Thus, my first evening as a "college prof" would be complete.

Personally, I always resented that first night script endorsed by the vast majority of college professors, but like most students, I accepted it. It always seemed frustrating to interrupt my evening activities (not that they were so productive) to travel to campus and be dismissed ten minutes later. After the first freshman semester, most students assumed that would be the routine and wouldn't bother to bring pencil or paper to the first class. Students learn that they are expected to be excited when early dismissal is announced, as if in elementary school a "snow-day" had been proclaimed. Insult was added to injury when a graduate student was assigned the "opening night task" and the lead professor reserved grand entrance rights for the second scheduled class session. I've always believed that in the event a substitute graduate assistant or GA served as a stand-in for the assigned professor, I should receive a rebate. This rebate would also apply if a class were cancelled, especially if the class was cancelled so the "professor could attend a conference." I'm not sure how that was ever a benefit to me.

Another one of my favorite rituals was an instructor who required seven textbooks for the course in an effort to convey the rigorous discipline needed to master the subject material. This instructor proceeded to casually reference two of the textbooks on three isolated occasions during the semester. Ultimately, the students would perform the ritual of returning the unopened books for a discounted refund. By the sophomore year, most students learned that writing their name in the front of the book would only reduce the amount of refund received; therefore, they avoided the ritual. The insult was only magnified when one of the required texts was authored by the instructor and written seventeen years ago when he or she was seeking tenure.

I don't consider myself to be a cynic of higher education; however, to say I am highly skeptical would be an understatement. I have taught at every level of education from high school to graduate school and served as a dean, vice provost, provost, and president of a college. I have witnessed most of the rituals and scams that are in play. The textbook scam mentioned is renewed annually and justified due to the reality that most students receive grants-in-aid; therefore, it "isn't really money out of their pockets." The reality of student loans resulting in massive student debt in the future is reserved for later discussion. The cost of textbooks pales in comparison to the cost of housing and tuition.

Escalating tuition cost goes unchecked because it usually requires state or system-wide approval, i.e., legislative approval. Legislators' grant approval because they don't want to defend an anti-education platform in their next campaign. Legislators are always readily aware of the quasi-united front that faculty represent. This remains a threat to legislators because faculty represent high voter turnout, may unite if threatened, and are very articulate in expressing their discontent should it be necessary. Isn't it just easier to go along with the flow? For independent institutions that don't require legislative approval for tuition hikes, it's easier to let the state institutions do the heavy lifting first and then adjust tuition upward in their shadow. It continues to be a vicious cycle with no end in sight.

Just a few more words on higher education prior to returning to the opening night class discussion. As an adjunct instructor, as well as the early years as a faculty member, it has been my observation that one does not immediately feel totally accepted by the fraternity of fellow faculty members. And this is to be expected. As an adjunct with limited resources, one is appreciative of the opportunity to share a secretary or possibly office space in order to post office hours (required but seldom honored). The primary concern of many instructors is to be within ten minutes of the scheduled class time and hopefully find a parking space. The other concern is to exit as fast as possible in order to return to their day job and trust that their absence has not been noticed.

For a newly appointed faculty member, the focus is on doing whatever is requested in order to "fit in" and to progress toward tenure. Although cordial, one's colleagues do not view the new faculty member as an equal for a variety of reasons. They are not sure of that person's commitment to the institution. This may be merely a steppingstone for one seeking appointment at a more prestigious school. Also, the newly appointed faculty members have not proven themselves by contributing publications to a "refereed journal." For the layperson, a "refereed journal" or publication reflects the content of a given discipline, and articles are reviewed and selected for publication by a committee of experts within the field. Many academics view this as the critical component contributing to tenure.

Initially as an adjunct gaining experience, and subsequently with my first full time faculty member appointment at another institution, I accepted this indifference and attributed it to the rookie experience. I was amused by the fact that three campus cars would be reserved for three faculty members all attending the same conference. The fact that many of the faculty members preferred to bring a sandwich from home and eat in the confines of their office with the door shut, opposed to dining in the faculty dining room, reflects this desire to withdraw.

As I entered the administrative ranks which required more intricate interaction among the faculty, I became aware of the fact that many of the faculty members didn't particularly care for one another. To suggest any social communication or supporting comment toward "The Administration" is flirting with the label of "traitor" to the faculty union. As I continued my progression through three community colleges and three universities, I realized this animosity between faculty and administration was not the exception but the rule.

This friction became more apparent as I began the scheduling of courses for the institution. Faculty were most cooperative and flexible with the scheduling of courses, provided their classes would meet between the hours of ten and two o'clock in the afternoon, on Monday, Wednesday, and Friday, if necessary. An evening class was acceptable, only if required in the contract. They were totally supportive of evening, weekend, and extension classes, providing they were not the ones assigned to teach the class. The faculty bristled at the suggestion that adjunct faculty members be hired to fill any available teaching slots. Adjunct faculty members were frequently seen as a threat to tenured faculty, primarily because they enjoyed students and the opportunity to teach.

Eventually it became very apparent that not only did the faculty not like each other or the administration, but they didn't care much for the students either, and by default, the institution as a whole. This observation was very bothersome to me early in my career prior to my exposure to two significant contributions from others who had walked in my shoes. The first was an article entitled, "A Discourse on Professorial Melancholia," written by David F. Machell and published in Community Review, by the City University of New York.

Machell does an excellent job of explaining how and why there is such a disconnect between faculty members and those to whom they are indebted. He succinctly outlines the journey to which most faculty members fall victim. Most faculty members aspire to join the profession because they have a deep-seated love for their discipline. Due to their junior status, new faculty are frequently assigned to teach the intro-level classes within the discipline, while the more intriguing topics are reserved for senior-level or graduate-level faculty. Unfortunately, the intro-level classes are frequently required classes; therefore, the bulk of attendees are students who have a marginal interest in the subject at best. The primary concern of the student is usually about test content only.

Secondly, the disappointment relating to the limited attention span of the freshman students is intensified by the lack of support from fellow faculty members. This along with extended commitments including committee participation and the need to publish or perish in order to influence tenure opportunities combine to form the perfect storm.

Let's return to the classroom.

SECTION IV

Leadership: Success/ Wealth/Fame

"*Of all the characteristics required of a leader, which one do you consider to be the most important?*"

"*That's a thought provoking question. Let's expand it to the class. I'd like to hear what you think.*" I was pleased to note the entire class was fully engaged at this point.

"*Charisma, Self-confidence, 'Visionary,*" came the responses.

"*Slow down; let me list them on the board,*" I pleaded and began the list:

Charisma
Self-confident
Visionary
Self-motivated
Creative
Trusting
Communicative
Intelligent
Humorous
Energetic
Optimistic

Leader

"*Does that do it?*" I questioned.

"*It's a good start,*" was the response.

"*Is it possible to find all of these traits in one person?*" I inquired.

"*Possibly, but rarely. If you did, that person would be a saint,*" was the response.

"*Perhaps that's the point that Rockefeller was trying to make. This combination of traits and the ability to lead is so rare it is virtually priceless.*"

What would it mean to an organization to *have someone at the helm with these characteristics?* I challenged.

"At least $480.00 an hour!" was the immediate answer.

"So here's your challenge. Utilizing your brain power along with that of two others sitting near you, assume you want this 'ideal CEO' but can't afford the million-a-year price tag. I want you to identify which two traits you would be willing to sacrifice in order to stay within budget and which one you consider to be absolutely essential. Select a spokesperson and we will hear your group's justification in fifteen minutes."

The room began to buzz with conversation as students began introducing themselves to their newly appointed teammates and began to jockey for reasons why they couldn't or shouldn't be the spokesperson for the group. In the hallway, I caught the eye of another rookie faculty member as he was exiting for the evening. He had this incredulous expression as he viewed the listing on the board and noticed the commotion of the students in the room.

I felt like I had broken some sort of sacred pedagogical pact by stepping out of the brotherhood and actually teaching the first night of class. I anticipated I would hear from the Dean that week and be reprimanded by the brotherhood. I didn't care, and I was feeling pretty good about what was taking place. The activity was no reflection of what I had planned for the first night, nor was there anything on the syllabus indicating any level of participation required, but I was feeling worthy to teach this special topics course, *Emerging Patterns of Leadership!*

"Who would like to begin?" I invited. Silence. *"All right, for five dollars, who knows the capital of Delaware?"* I advanced the five dollars from my pocket and a hand immediately shot up and simultaneously called out, *"Dover."*

"Would anyone like to challenge that?" I petitioned. *"Hearing no objections, may I ask your name?"*

"Glenn Wright"

"Well, thank you, Mr. Wright. That answer provides you with two opportunities. First, the five dollars is yours, and secondly, you have the opportunity

to represent your group and share your choice of the traits you would be willing to sacrifice in a CEO and also that one trait you deem absolutely essential."

"May I be creative in my response and suggest I only receive four dollars and another group go first?" he responded. The class laughed and cheered his response as he made his way to the front of the room.

"No deal, but good try." I offered. *"How did you know Dover?"* I asked.

"My grandmother lives there and we made the journey every summer since I was knee high to a grasshopper," he offered.

"Sounds reasonable. Please, share with us what your group came up with, Mr. Wright."

"After much deliberation and in order to have some response, we decided self-confidence and self-motivation were the two traits we were willing to sacrifice in the CEO." The murmurs of disagreement were audible.

"Hang on. You'll get your chance," I coached. *"How did you and your group come to this conclusion, Mr. Wright?"* I needled.

"We considered these two traits possible by-products or end products that may not be essential up front, but given time and some opportunities for success, they were traits that would be developed and acquired?" he urged.

"So, would that be a question or a statement, Mr. Wright?" I quizzed.

"Let's see. I already have the five dollars, don't I?" Laughter and I nodded. *"That being the case, I would like to offer that up as a statement of fact,"* Wright inserted.

"Would anyone like to refute that?" I hinted.

"What makes you think there would be any success without those traits?" a voice from the back.

"And your name is?" I asked.

"Brittany Reynolds," she responded.

"Thank you, Miss Reynolds. Mr. Wright, it's all yours."

"Yea, well, we had a problem with that also."

"Jeff, another member of our group also had some concerns."

"Please identify yourself, Jeff." He raised his hand and we applauded.

"Well, perhaps Jeff can explain it better." It was obvious Jeff was caught off guard, as he made his way to the front. *"Or as they say, it's all yours, Jeff."*

"Thanks, Glenn. I'll remember this."

"Well, we looked at success from a different perspective and concluded; most people would consider winning the lottery or driving to work and arriving on time as successful ventures. Both activities can be completed successfully and don't require any measurable degree of self-confidence or self-motivation. However, accomplishing either or both, over a given amount of time, would no doubt be considered a success, and both traits would grow over time but not be necessary initially.

Glenn jumped back in. *"Or think of a pro athlete or accomplished musician. They may have a raw talent, but lack confidence or motivation; however, after they compete on several occasions, both traits may become clearly obvious."* This response generated a rowdy applause for the two. With ample grins of satisfaction, they shook hands and began their exit to their seats.

"Excellent. And may I pause for a teaching moment?" I urged at the same time I took center stage. *"Let me ask this. Did either Glenn's or Jeff's self-confidence grow as a result of that exchange?"* Most nodded approvingly. *"So we would consider this a successful experience for them?"* More agreement from the class

"Now consider this. Was there any evidence of self-motivation on their part prior to be being selected, aside from Glenn's desire for the five dollars?" Most indicated no. *"Therefore, a successful outcome with limited or no evidence of self-confidence or self-motivation. Perhaps they proved their own point? Now, if you wouldn't mind, we are curious which trait your group thought was absolutely essential in your ideal CEO?"*

"Take it away, Robin," Glenn volunteered. She made her way forward.

"We also found this task rather challenging. However, we did have unanimous agreement. We agreed that none of it would work if the person at the top didn't have a sense of humor." The class cheered; it was obvious there was agreement with her selection.

Each group voiced their conclusion. There were a variety of traits selected that the groups felt were not essential in order for a CEO to lead successfully. The justification for elimination was usually anchored in the belief that the benefit of a given trait could be purchased within the character of another employee. This trait would then be available to the CEO as needed. For example, vision could be purchased in the form of a futurist. Creativity in its various forms may be found in local artists. Intelligence could be sub-contracted from the regional university by utilizing its resources in research and development. Integrity was viewed as a by-product of a successful administration, much like confidence and motivation. Trustworthiness also fell under this justification. Effective communication could be accomplished by having the right assistant or well- groomed public relations office.

As the discussion continued, it became apparent that many students felt current CEOs were in fact being protected by having good people running interference for them. Several examples were cited of prominent CEOs and officials who were once held in high esteem and only revealed at the bewitching hour as the corruption, fraud, embezzlement, and incompetence were revealed prior to some form of investigation or bankruptcy.

Desirable personal characteristics in the form of charismatic optimism and moral crusades were frequently revealed as shams or counterfeit imitations of uncontrollable narcissism. The conversation relating to trustfulness in personal or professional relationships began to suggest these traits no longer existed. It was time for me to step in. *"Let us shift our focus from those desirable but expendable traits to the one trait that virtually every group identified as the essential trait of an effective CEO: a sense of humor. When we get back from our break, we will discuss this elusive trait. However, before you go, I would like everyone to take a scrap of paper, borrow from your neighbor if necessary, and rate what you consider your sense of humor to be using a one-to-ten scale, with one being low and ten being high. Please drop that on my desk on your way out. Take fifteen; you deserve it."*

SECTION V

A Sense of Humor

Unbeknownst to the students and certainly not what I had planned for the evening, we had drifted into an area of interest where I had considerable expertise and comfort. I have always been fascinated by the concepts of effective leaders and leadership and what makes them unique. A sense of humor is frequently cited as an essential trait, and I had invested considerable time and energy in my graduate studies chasing this elusive trait. It was now time to investigate some of the theories I had developed and get feedback from a vocal group. I was enjoying the evening immensely and sensed the students were also by the quality of the discussion in class as well as their interaction with each other during break. I suffered no guilt over my lack of focus, realizing everyone else who had scheduled a Monday night class was already home watching football. This was fun.

"Welcome back. Before you get settled in, I would ask that you would complete one more task. Please take another piece of paper, and if you are currently working or reflecting on a previous boss, evaluate that person's sense of humor utilizing the same one-to-ten scale you used to evaluate yourself. Please pass your scores to the right, and Kim, would you please total these and calculate an average for us?"

"While you were on break, I had the opportunity to calculate the class average. I'm curious, what do you think it was?" The responses ranged from a low of four to a high of nine.

"Survey says, seven point zero." I reported. *"Now Kim, what did our bosses average?"*

"Survey says, three point seven five." A big gasp from the class was evident.

"There you have it. We tend to rate ourselves very high and those we work for very low. Psychologists would say this is a protective measure on our part because psychologically it would be very damaging to our self-esteem if we concluded we were very low on the scale, or without a sense of humor."

"First of all, let me say your results are very similar to a variety of audiences surveyed before. First let me ask, was this a difficult decision for anyone,

evaluating either your or your boss' sense of humor?" They all agreed it was not a problem.

"Secondly, what criteria did you use to determine your scores?" Silence prevailed. *"Think about this. If you were requested to estimate weight, height, or even IQ, you would have an established frame of reference or scale of some sort. Let's look at the other senses. Whether it is sight, smell, taste, touch, or hearing, we have instruments to measure it to a one minute decibel. And yet, we are quick to evaluate ourselves and others in reference to a sense of humor with no tangible base of reference. Why is that?"* I did not wait for a response. I knew it was not forthcoming.

"This is the question that is rarely asked and never resolved, and yet understanding this trait lies at the very foundation of comprehending leadership. Not only is it critical to one's professional success, it is the number one characteristic desired by both men and women in a significant other. And we don't agree on that much.

Let's first ask the question, is it truly a 'sense' in the purest form? If we consult Webster, sense is defined as 'a bodily function or mechanism involving the action and effect of a stimulus on a sense organ.' If we consider a sense of humor in context with the other senses, the inconsistency jumps out. It is easy to identify the sense organ associated with any of the other senses: sight, smell, taste, hearing and feel/touch. And the organ associated with humor? Non-existent. In short, it is a stretch to identify humor as a sense at all."

"However, let's not get hung up on the semantics and whether or not it is a sense. Let's just talk about what it is. So please, I know you have some opinions. You tell me what it is, and I'll do my best to capture your thoughts on the board. Who's first?"

"Well, it's kind of hard to explain. It's one of those things, you know it when you see it," was the first contribution.

"Okay, what I'm hearing is, it's mysterious and subjective." I listed those on the board.

"Yea, it's like success. You know it when you see it," he offered.

Another student jumped in. *"Hang on. I don't think success is mysterious or subjective. Show me your checkbook, and I'll tell you on the spot if you are successful."* We all laughed.

"Is there anyone in here who doesn't think Bill Gates is successful?" I asked.

"I'm not sure," was a voice from the back.

"And you are?" I inquired.

"MaryAnn Jacobs," she responded.

"Okay, Miss Jacobs. Why do you hesitate to acknowledge Bill Gates as a success?" I asked.

"Well, because we really don't know who Bill Gates is. We know he's good at making money and he appears to be pretty smart, but we don't know who he is behind closed doors. And I think that's more important in determining if someone is a success or not." Applause from the class rang out.

"It sounds like you have some supporters here, Miss Jacobs," I offered.

"Well, thank you. I need all the help I can get," she responded with a laugh.

"I'm hearing support for both mysterious and subjective. Is there another descriptive word that defines what a sense of humor is? Is success in some form a prerequisite for a sense of humor? Before we move on, let's define success. If you don't mind, young man, reach your left arm out and grab that dictionary sitting on the bookcase and let us know how success is defined.

"Will do, and my name is Rick Myers in the event you are recording extra credit points," he gained class support as he began flipping pages. *"Here we go, success; a favorable or desired outcome. Second definition of success is the gaining of wealth and fame."*

"According to this definition, Bill Gates certainly deserves the designation of success on both accounts. How about Mother Teresa? Does she qualify as a success?

A resounding yes from the class. *"She certainly had the fame."* I observed. *"Did she have a sense of humor?"* The lack of response was indicative that none of us felt comfortable with attaching the label of humor to Mother Teresa because of our limited exposure to her.

"So, what's the consensus? Is humor, as we have defined it, a characteristic of success?"

"No, absolutely not!" *"There are too many examples of people with a great sense of humor that are neither wealthy nor famous,"* were the responses.

"So let's refocus. In addition to being mysterious and subjective and not necessarily reserved for 'successful' people, what other descriptive words do we have to define this desirable trait? Note, I didn't call it a sense," I offered.

"It makes you feel better when you are around them. I'm not sure what you would call that?

"Contagious?"

"Thank you, Carol. Is there agreement with this? Should I add it to the list?" The class offered unanimous support.

"To me a certain irony exists here. We have identified that the most desirable trait in a CEO or a leader or in a significant other is a sense of humor. We have further clarified that it truly is not a 'sense' at all, and the best description we can come up with is that this desirable trait is mysterious, subjective, and contagious. A rather soft definition if you ask me, and yet, we are very quick to evaluate to what extent or degree this trait is present not only in ourselves but others as well."

"Here is your assignment for next week. First, I would like you to pick up a syllabus for next week on your way out. Please note the required textbook listed and the reading assignment."

"Also for next week. Obviously, we have given a lot of weight or credibility to the importance or significance of a sense of humor as it relates to leadership and by inference, upward mobility. I would like you to bring in anecdotal examples of 'successful' people displaying humor. Secondly, bring two contributions from credible sources that would either support or refute this elevated status we have granted to humor."

***

"Welcome back. I trust you had a good and prosperous week. I was pleased from the message I received from the registrar's office that no one dropped the class and that we have added a few to max out the enrollment. To those brave souls joining us tonight, I offer a warm welcome. I would also remind you that the opportunity to drop or add a class ends this Wednesday, in the event you may have overlooked the fact that this class does take place during Monday night football." Some feigned disappointment and scooted their chairs as if they were going to exit which generated a chuckle from the class.

"All right, don't say I didn't warn you. My name is Jim Haviland and the class is entitled, Emerging Patterns of Leadership. Here is the syllabus, which has provided very little guidance, if last week is any indication. Please raise your hand if you need one, and we will be underway."

I continued. *"In an effort to bring you up to date, we became a little side tracked trying to identify why some leaders or CEOs were paid in excess of $400 an hour, I believe, calculated by Mr. Wright by dividing $1,000,000 by the standard 2080, the number of work hours in a year, given a forty-hour work week. We concluded CEOs possessed some personality traits that may justify this generous salary. Now class, help me out; you say the desired trait, and I will list them on the board again."* The students called them out one at a time.

"After considerable discussion, we concluded that many of these traits may possibly be provided by other key staff members, but the one trait that is absolutely essential for success and incidentally the same trait we seek in a significant other and that is? Help me out, class."

"A sense of humor," was delivered in unison.

"We then made two other significant findings. One, that a sense of humor is essentially not a 'sense' in its purest form, unlike the other 'senses' linked to a particular body organism, like a sense of taste would be associated with the tongue. Secondly, we concluded, it is difficult to pin down precisely what a sense of humor was, although we know it when we see it. Then, much to our embarrassment, we realized we were quick to rate ourselves and others on a one-to-ten rating scale, the degree to which this trait was present, although admittedly the trait was mysterious, subjective, and contagious."

"So in short, you didn't miss a thing." Laughter throughout the class. *"Oh and one more thing,"* I added. *"We concluded that success in our culture was defined by wealth and fame, although we recognized that it was possible to be considered successful without acquiring wealth or fame."*

"What would be an example of that, where success was achieved without those outcomes?" One of the new students asked.

"Let's see. I think we referred to Mother Teresa. However, she did achieve fame, and it could be argued that innocuous lottery-winners would be considered successful by most people, but hang on; it may simply be the fact that they have now achieved fame that makes them 'successful'." I was struggling for clarification.

"I know. Take a parent or couple who have who have raised a good child or family. I think most people would identify that achievement as 'successful,' and yet there is no wealth or fame attached to it."

"Now that I think of it, it makes you wonder, is that why so many people have

kids? Is raising a good family one of the more commonly and readily acceptable ways of obtaining success, but not necessarily achieving wealth and fame?"

"In any event, I have asked that you bring in examples of humor demonstrated by 'successful' people and also some definitions of leaders or leadership which will be shared later. However, prior to that, I would like to confuse the issue even more.

Therefore, does it confuse the issue if I say, be aware that humor has little to do with jokes or comedy?" Mass confusion and looks of perplexity prevailed.

"Let me explain," I urged. *"I had the opportunity to consult William Funk's work, Word Origins and Their Romantic Stories. According to Funk, we borrow the term 'humour' bodily from the Latin. Ancient philosophers believed that the mixture of four fluids within our bodies was essential to determining one's health.* (Much like today's blood sample reveals so much of what is happening internally.) *The mixture, color and texture of blood, phlegm, bile, and black bile were the key to determining one's health. So how does this relate to one's sense of humor? It may simply be a matter of convenience and evolution of terms regarding the merger of two dynamics. The Latin word for liquid is 'humor,' and the Latin word for mixture is 'temperamentum'. In short, if the mixture (temperamentum) of these four liquids (humors) was satisfactory in color and texture, one was considered healthy or to have a humorous temperament. Please note having a humorous temperament has nothing to do with jokes, one's ability to tell jokes, or comedy. It has to do with being healthy, and it doesn't stretch one's imagination much to see how other behaviors consistent with a humorous temperament like smiling, laughing, and likeability would over time be associated with jokes and comedy. Humor has nothing to do with jokes and comedy."*

"It is a disposition, and acknowledging it in this form explains why it is so mysterious and subjective in nature. It also explains why it is contagious. We have a tendency to smile back at those smiling at us, and we have all witnessed how one infectious laugh may spread throughout an entire theatre.

"So let me recap. We have determined that a sense of humor is a desirable trait. We have also concluded that this trait is not a 'sense' in the purest form, and now we have the revelation that it has nothing to do with jokes or comedy as commonly believed. So how are we doing?"

"What was the ending date for that 'drop-add period' you mentioned?" A brave soul ventured much to the enjoyment of the rest of the class.

"So, with that being said, who would like to share their anecdotal example of humor?" I challenged.

"I'll give it a shot," student Mike Ridgeway offered. *"When Lee Iacocca, a non-candidate for President, was constantly badgered by the press regarding the possibility of a potential candidacy, he quipped, 'I have no political ambitions and would appreciate a different line of questioning.' He added further clarification, 'I find that line of questioning tiresome, and besides, it makes my campaign manager nervous.'* The magazine article states the room erupted in laughter."

"I'll go," Mary Ann jumped in. *"When Senator Douglas accused Abe Lincoln of being a hypocrite, wishy-washy, and two-faced, Lincoln won the crowd over by declaring; 'I've just been accused of being two-faced. Now I ask you, if I had two faces, would I pick this one?'* We all know the end result."

"My turn, here's one I heard the other night."

"A man was driving down the street in a sweat because he had an important meeting and couldn't find parking. Looking up toward heaven, he said, 'Lord, take pity on me. If you find me a parking space, I will go to church every Sunday for the rest of my life and give up drinking.' Miraculously, a parking space appeared. The man looked up again and said, 'Never mind. I found one.'" Good response from the class. More moans than not.

Glenn Wright got philosophical on us. *"I looked up jokes at the library and came up with this. The bride was disappointed when introduced to the prospective groom. 'Why have you brought me here?' she asked reproachfully. 'He's ugly and old, he squints and has bad teeth and bleary eyes ...' 'You needn't lower your voice,' interrupted the broker. He's deaf as well."* Moans throughout the room.

He continued, *"That was taken from Sigmund Freud's work, Jokes and the Unconscious. I must admit I found the book rather fascinating, before I got in over my head. If I understood what he was saying, man experiences conflict as he simultaneously seeks pleasure while avoiding criticism. Jokes provide a release from that tension by providing an avenue to experience the desired pleasure and limit the possibility of criticism.*

"I quit reading when the topic of alcohol was introduced, because I was going out later. Apparently alcohol reduces the inhibiting forces, criticism among them, and makes pleasure more accessible. Two other things, if I may? Freud did quote

a guy, Lipps? He agreed with what we had said in class about humor being totally subjective. I found the discussion about how both conflict and tension coexist, and humor provides a release value very interesting. I mean, how many times have we heard somebody say, 'It was just a joke,' as justification when somebody takes offense? I recalled how ballistic that comedian from the Seinfeld show acted by increasing racial slurs in his act even when the racially-mixed audience wasn't buying into his material. It made me realize how closely related humor or jokes may be to hostility or aggression."

I contributed. *"I do believe Freud went on to say, that which we laugh at the loudest may be an indication of where our personal tension or aggression may be the most intense. For example, someone who resents his boss may laugh the loudest at the joke, 'My boss' definition of long-range planning is where to go for lunch.' And we all have seen 'straights' laugh hilariously at 'gay' jokes. I believe Freud would suggest, what lies at the unconscious level may be far more revealing than we would like to think."*

"Thanks, Glenn. That was great." I complimented.

"One more thing, Dr. Haviland, if I may?"

"Surely," I responded.

"I hate that when people call me Shirley," (cheap, but thoroughly enjoyed by all of us).

"Yes, Mr. Wright. What would you like to add?"

"I just had an epiphany," he declared.

"Please share," I encouraged.

"When Freud said we would seek pleasure and avoid criticism, he was right. In the form of confession, I would like to admit in my earlier joke about the wedding couple; I switched the joke to be on the bridegroom rather than on the bride. Why? When I anticipated telling the joke tonight in class, I thought there might be criticism if the victim were the bride and not the groom, as I told it. I wanted the pleasure of telling the joke but avoiding any possible criticism. I think that Freud guy may have been a pretty bright guy."

Applause and laughter.

"He had his moments," I agreed.

As the commotion died, *"On that note, I should jump in. As the son of a preacher man, I know I've heard all of the jokes,"* he said jokingly. *"When*

I mentioned our assignment to my father, the preacher, he referenced a book by Eldon Trueblood, The Humor of Christ."

"I told him I wasn't aware of any examples of humor by Christ. He said, most people weren't, but it can be found in the parables. When Christ made reference to the unlikelihood of a camel getting through the eye of a needle, it would be analogous to a contemporary speaker referring to a snowball's chance in hell."

Interesting perspective. When indications or examples of humor are taken out of context or aided by the distortions of time, the impact is lost. I don't imagine the insertion of "Where's the beef?" would get much response from a contemporary audience. However, this quote from a very popular Wendy's Restaurant commercial was pivotal when delivered by candidate Walter Mondale and directed toward candidate Gary Hart.

Freud also referred to this, indicating most jokes have a timely topicality and are frequently dependent upon a wide variety of experiences and exposure. I'm reminded of the quips Bush Sr. made when running against Michael Dukakis when he said,

"Dukakis's foreign affairs experience amounts to eating breakfast once at the International House of Pancakes," in addition to his line, *"Dukakis thinks a foreign market is a place where you go to buy French bread."* In order to completely enjoy that line, a certain degree of exposure would be desirable opposed to offering a 'knock-knock' joke.

This dependency on exposure and timeliness may explain a degree of sophistication necessary to appreciate some jokes and double meanings offered by comedians. It certainly would explain why some elderly people may appear to be humorless. It may simply be the fact that isolation from worldly events may be the true culprit.

"I have a political example also," offered another student. *"When John F. Kennedy was running against Hubert Humphrey, he said, 'Hubert's problem is that he has too many ideas and too much energy. He alarms the country. I think the people want a less controversial and more boring candidate, someone like me.'*

"According to Gerald Gardner, author of All the Presidents' Wit, 'it's a toss-up between Kennedy and Regan. Both have been very adroit in using humor to ingratiate themselves and to defuse sensitive issues. Kennedy was willing to

make fun of his Catholicism, wealth, and inexperience as he pursued the highest office in the land.'"

"I found an interesting one. In Mark McCormick's book, What They Didn't Teach You at Harvard Business School, he cites a sense of humor as the second most important trait necessary for success. The first? Common sense."

Following contributions from about fifty percent of the class, I abruptly inserted, *"So what do you think? Did we hear some good examples of humor in action?"* Most nodded approvingly.

"I don't think so," offered one of the newly added students.

"And you would be?" I asked.

"Marcie Grimes."

"Okay, Miss Grimes. Tell us what you're thinking," I encouraged.

"Well, if I understand what you said earlier, humor is a disposition and what we have just heard are jokes or examples of comedy."

"Bingo." I responded. *"You're right on target. Now, if the response from Lincoln regarding his two faces was an off-the-cuff original, which it may have been, it would be considered a spontaneous and non-defensive remark, therefore indicative of his disposition. On the other hand, if his response is part of his scripted repertoire relating to his flip-flop on issues, it would be considered a joke or attempt at comedy. There is a big difference, one being a sincere reflection of disposition, the other, a sound bite of who the man wants you to think he is. It's very hard to distinguish between the two given an isolated example because the lack of sincerity may be camouflaged in its delivery."* A pause to allow for reflection.

"Not to confuse the issue even more, but frequently the desired end result, audience approval, may be the same regardless if it is a true reflection of the person's disposition or merely manipulation of the audience.

In an earlier life (many years ago), I worked celebrity security for the MGM Grand Hotel in Las Vegas. I remember standing side stage during Dean Martin's early show at 8:00 p.m. My only exposure to the man prior to this was via television like most people. I was aware of his reputation of being quite the drinker only by way of gossip and the mockery he made of himself in the skits he performed.

The truth is, he drank only orange juice before the show and then poured a glass of water with a twist of lime as he was being introduced. Upon introduction, he staggered unto the stage acting totally inebriated and disoriented. Midway he yelled out, "LOOK OUT!" pointing upward toward the single spotlight focused on him in a dark auditorium. "Oh my God, I thought it was a train." And it did look like that, and the audience roared. I remember saying to myself, "Boy, this guy is good, totally spontaneous."

I held that belief until approximately 10:05 p.m. that evening, when the second show began, complete with the twist of lime, the staggering walk and "LOOK OUT!" I remember I felt like a stooge. I felt I had been had. There wasn't one ounce of spontaneity in that entire performance. Every gesture, every raised eyebrow, and every belly-laugh, fully orchestrated and rehearsed. The fact that he was able to pull it off so well, night after night, was a testimony to his professionalism and also a lesson in life for me.

The 2008 presidential election provides some immediate examples of this dynamic. *"What is the difference between a hockey mom and a pit bull?"* A line delivered by Sarah Palin as she viewed hockey mom signs in front of her (pause); *"Lipstick."* And the crowd erupted in applause. I would suggest that was a scripted or coached line, a joke. However, the delivery was flawless and appeared spontaneous. It endeared her, possibly for a lifetime, to millions of Americans.

Mike Hucklebee received a similar bump in the polls during the primaries when asked, "What would Jesus do if he were in a similar situation?" And Mike responded (paraphrased), *"First of all, he wouldn't be stupid enough to run for public office."* Deafening laughter and applause from the class.

I believe by virtue of his body language and facial expression, he was caught totally off guard by the question, which made his response all the more impactful because it appeared spontaneous, unrehearsed, and unscripted.

His trip to the mountaintop was short lived. In the days immediately following the debates, it was obvious he thought he had struck a vein with the American voters and began inserting witticism at virtually every stump speech. *"He may not be able to part the Red Sea, but he was able to part the red tape in Washington."* The scripted and rehearsed one-liners came across as being insincere and ingenuous. It was the difference between evident spontaneous humor demonstrated in the debate and the canned predictability of rehearsed jokes.

John McCain's ill advised, *"Bomb, Bomb, Bomb Iran"* opening was another failed attempt to appear spontaneous by inserting scripted material orchestrated to get a laugh. These failed attempts frequently leave an audience perplexed trying to figure out who is the real person.

"Let's refocus with some more examples with one additional dimension. Let's try to evaluate the example and categorize it as either an example of humor or jokes and comedy. Better yet, let's get rid of that word comedy in the discussion, and we have Funk to thank for that explanation also. According to Wilfred Funk, the origin of the word comedy stems from the Greece of two millenniums ago. A 'komos' was a festival. The chief singer at the festival, the Komoidos, eventually evolved to comedian, and we derive the word comedy. So give your example, and we will categorize in one of the two columns on the board. Is it evidence of humor or a joke?"

Virtually all the remaining examples were categorized as jokes opposed to true indications of humor. Ronald Regan provided some interesting conversations with several examples of his wit offered as evidence of humor. Without a doubt, the favorite was his response to Walter Mondale's reference to Regan's advanced age in the second debate. Regan's response was; "I will not make age an issue in this campaign. I am not going to exploit, for political purposes, my opponent's youth and inexperience." Even Mondale laughed. However, more importantly, they never returned to the issue again.

Another telling comment coming from Regan was his remark to the surgeons as he was placed on the operating table after being shot, *"I hope you're all Republicans."* We have no way of knowing if the age response was rehearsed; one would suspect so. However, it is highly unlikely that the comment in the operating room was rehearsed given the timing and the immediacy of the action. Ronald Reagan ended his term of office with the highest approval rating of any president since Franklin Roosevelt.

The irony is that Regan received negative ratings for his handling of every social issue posted: civil rights; 51 percent negative, education; 54 percent negative, housing; 65 percent negative, and welfare; 67 percent negative. On the other hand, the same survey noted two-thirds of the responses rated his leadership ability as excellent or good. Three-quarters favorably rated his charisma and ability to communicate.

Many students chose Reagan as their selected example of one demonstrating an effective use of humor. Perhaps that contributed to Reagan being recognized as "The Great Communicator." Reagan was also a dedicated student in the study of Abraham Lincoln, another successful individual who was frequently cited as possessing a keen sense of humor.

One of my favorite comments about Lincoln was offered by Peter Wyden in his biography of Iacocca, who was making the equivalent of $8,653.85 per hour at the height of his career ($17.9 million annually) with Chrysler. Incidentally, when Iacocca was confronted by the press when his substantial salary was revealed, he responded, *"I was embarrassed,"* he said. *"But what should I do? Should I root for the stock to go down?"*

In reference to Regan, Iacocca states, *"You know, in life there are some people you meet whom you'd just like to pal around with. They're fun, they put you in a good frame of mind, and they make you feel terrific. Well, that's Ronald Regan."* Iacocca later adds, *"There's no way on earth you could dislike him."*

Following the break, the balance of the evening was consumed by sharing various definitions of leadership that had been found from over 600 definitions available, according to Burns. The class favorite was, *"Leadership is the ability to be out of control comfortably."*

It had been a most stimulating evening. *"Next week, we will scrutinize this critical trait more closely. We will examine not only the origins of humor, or should I say a humorous disposition, but the value of this disposition as it relates to leadership. We will examine what happens to it and how one may regain it. Keep up with your reading, and have a good week."*

***

"Well, welcome back. I trust everyone had a good week, and we welcome the new students who have joined us during the drop and add period. I am Jim Haviland, the instructor of this class entitled 'Emerging Patterns of Leadership,' and I am the one responsible for leading this class on a wild goose chase over the past few weeks."

"Allow me to bring you up to date. We began discussing why it is that some people make so much more money than others with apparently the same qualifications. We concluded it was due to personality, and then went on to document some of Carnegie's work that states as much as 85% of one's success directly attributed to one's personality, regardless of the occupation."

"Incidentally, class, I think you will find something similar to this finding in Malcolm Gladwell's recent book, Blink. He presents the case of an insurance company seeking to find out who, among all the physicians covered by the company, is most likely to be sued for malpractice. What they found out was the risk of being sued had very little to do with how many mistakes a doctor makes. The major factor that influenced whether or not a suit was initiated was how the patient was treated on a personal level by their doctor. The difference was entirely in how they talked to their patients. Again we are back to personality, and the medical community just happens to have another word for personality as it applies to physicians: bedside manner. We went on to identify several traits consistent with leadership such as charisma, self-confidence, etc. and then did a forced choice to determine which of these traits are not essential, primarily because they can be found in competent assistants. These traits range from intelligence to creativity. However, we concluded that a sense of humor was critical for success at the executive level."

"We then rated ourselves on a one to ten scale, with ten being the highest, what we perceived our own sense of humor to be. And the class average was?"

"Seven-point-five," the class chimed in.

"And why was that significant, Marcie?"

"Because we then submitted what we perceived our bosses' humor to be, and it was much lower. I believe the average was right around four."

"And why was that important?" I inquired.

"Because it demonstrated either we were rating ourselves too high, or it was just a coincidence that all of us had bosses that were losers. But more importantly, we discussed how willingly we evaluate both ourselves and others on a trait where

no benchmark for accurate measurement exists. This was even more awkward when we realized all the other senses have finely tuned instrumentation for measuring the acuteness of them."

"Excellent, Marcie."

"Now, Mike perhaps you could elaborate on the balance of our discussion for the benefit of the new students?"

"Sure. We looked at the definitions of humor to find out that it had nothing to do with jokes or comedy but was a medical evaluation of one's overall health as a result of mixing bodily fluids, also known as humors in Latin or Greek. I'm not sure which one it was. It is really more of a disposition than it is a trait."

"Any other definitions come to mind? Yes, Robin."

"We defined success as a favorable or desired outcome and secondly as gaining wealth and fame."

"And did that clear up the matter?" I asked.

"No, it only made it more confusing," offered Kim.

"Why was that?" I asked.

"Because it was pointed out that many people are considered successful but have neither wealth nor fame. I believe the example was couples or individuals who have done a good job parenting would be considered successful, but little wealth or fame as a result."

"Did we elaborate on any other characteristics of this trait?" I led.

"We said it was mysterious, subjective, and contagious," offered Brittany.

"Can anyone think of any examples we cited as demonstrating this mysterious trait?"

I heard, *"Reagan, Lincoln, Christ, Iacocca, and Palin."*

"Anyone recall Iacocca's salary at the time he was getting all the favorable press?" I asked.

"Over eight thousand dollars an hour!" several students offered.

"Might be worth taking a look at what makes a guy worth that much." I suggested. *"By the way I saw my department chairman this week and told him our class had taken a detour from patterns of leadership to the most important trait of leadership, and he gave it his blessing. I thought you should know,"* I confessed.

"Okay, excellent review."

"Now let's pick up the discussion from there. And let me approach some of the

new blood that has arrived tonight and has not been contaminated by our previous discussions. Young lady in the red, may I ask your name?"

"Chrystal Shannon," she volunteered.

"Miss Shannon. Where do you think this mysterious trait of humor comes from?

"I would guess one is born with it" she offered.

"Are you from a large family, Miss Shannon?" I asked.

"I have two brothers and a sister" she said.

"Not to be presumptuous, but may I assume they are all from the same parents?"

"You may," she responded

"And would you say you all have a similar sense of humor?"

"Absolutely not," she quickly responded.

"Really? If you had to rate them independently and also yourself on a one to ten scale, how would you rate them?

She paused and wrote down some numbers. *"As you indicated during the review, I would rate myself about an eight, my oldest brother a seven, my sister a four and my youngest brother a two and I'm being generous with that."* That got a good laugh from her classmates. I believe they could identify with the family dynamics.

"Has it always been that way?" I asked.

She hesitated. *"No, I don't think so. As a matter of fact, I think we all got along well until my youngest brother hit middle school and he became a visitor from another planet."* We all laughed.

"So let's put this in perspective," I suggested. *"You indicated you came from the same parents, you believe each individual was born with a sense of humor intact, and yet there is a large range in your scoring of your siblings' humor, with you rating yourself the highest. Is that correct?"*

"Yea, but I don't like the way it sounds when you say it." Laughter. *"I guess what I'm trying to say is, it seems we all have a genetic makeup that contributes to our overall sense of humor, but regardless of the similarity in genetic makeup something happens in the home environment that has a tremendous influence on the final disposition of each individual. For my brother, when he went to middle school, it seemed like the transition had more of an influence on him than our home environment including my parents."*

"Do you think it was the physical move to a new building or facility that had the impact, or the fact that he was confronted with the adjusting to a new peer group?" I queried.

"I would guess it had more to do with making new friends and the entire adjustment of changing classes every hour, trying to fit in with a much larger group, the pressure of competing for a place on the team and his first exposure to mixed dances and all the pressure that goes with that," she volunteered. *"Now I'm starting to feel guilty that I wasn't more patient with him during that period."* Laughter and a lot of head nods from classmates that could identify with what she had to say.

"Why should you feel guilty? You had to make the same adjustment?" I challenged.

"Yea, but I had my older brother who was already attending the middle school there to walk in with me every day. And I made the cheerleading squad within the first two weeks of school along with my best friend from elementary school. And now that I think of it, we were both invited to the first social dance event, and my younger brother couldn't get up the nerve to ask a girl to go when he was there."

"What conclusions can you draw from these experiences that relate back to our discussion of humor?" I was searching.

"Although it appears to be a level playing field, and for the most part it probably is, as we are children growing up in the same home environment, however very early in our development, other factors begin to have as much, if not more influence than our own parents," Chrystal volunteered.

"Excellent observation and summation, Chrystal. And I think you will find a plethora of research in both psychology and sociology that will support the observations that you have made regarding the influence of the parents and the home environment as well as the peer group. Now combine the insecurities that come with a changing body and personality with the influences of birth order within a family and all the variables that affect the disposition of the parents as well as the other siblings in the home environment, and we begin to realize the complexities that contribute to what we commonly refer to as one's sense of humor or the existence of a humorous trait. Let's take a break," I offered.

"Dr. Haviland, before we do, I have one question," from Rick Myers. *"Shoot,"* I responded. *"This plethora thing, is that a good thing or a bad thing?"* Explosive laughter from the class. I was pleased how this

semester was shaping up. This was a group of bright and highly motivated students eager to learn. I couldn't wait to return from break.

Over break, I had the opportunity to reflect on two experiences I had earlier in my career as I began my quest to identify what makes one person so much more successful than another. Carnegie's work regarding the importance of personality had a huge impact on me, and then I was confronted with the dilemma similar to what I had just experienced in class. If two people from the same household had such differences in disposition and considerable research had identified the home environment and peer group as being critical influences, at what age did this transition begin to stifle what appeared to be a very spontaneous and creative disposition of a child? I found my answer.

SECTION VI

Risk/Self-Esteem

During the first five years of my oldest son's life, I cherished his creative works of art, reassuring him that there may be dogs that have wheels and cars with wings. As he entered kindergarten, I eagerly examined his work every evening wanting to enjoy the learning process with him. Reflecting on his day, he shared that they had to draw a tree and then tell the class about their tree. He eagerly showed his tree. It was a multicolored tree with a variety of colored leaves in the foliage and similar colored leaves lying at the base of the tree, obviously representing a fall landscape.

When I asked what he said to explain his tree to the class, his pride disappeared, and he attempted to dismiss my question by indicating four other students had gone before him. I acknowledged that, however, but was persistent in wanting to hear his explanation of his tree. And then the truth came out. With lowered eyes and a quivering lip, he went on to explain that the first four students the teacher had called upon had very similar trees; they all had a straight trunk with a green tuft of leaves at the top, commonly referred to as the "lollipop" tree. And then she called on my son. He said he didn't do it. In our society we would rather say we didn't do it than to look different from the others. It's called conformity, and in a larger arena, it is called the process of socialization.

I had an opportunity to witness the extent of this socialization process later in the year. I was teaching a vacation Bible school class and had to teach a twenty minute lesson to three different age groups. There were elementary-age students in one group, middle and high school in a second group and adults in the third. I approached each group as if there were a camera in the back of the classroom and I was filming three takes with the same introduction lines in order to experience their reaction. I entered the room with the elementary kids and casually announced, "I need a volunteer." And total bedlam broke out as kids jockeyed for position vigorously waving their hands and screaming "Pick me, pick me," at the top of their voices, believing the closer their hands were to my face the more likely they were to be chosen. And tremendous disappointment echoed about as those left standing witnessed the selection of two energetic volunteers. Those not selected slowly shuffled back to their seats with heads bowed wondering how the world could be so cruel.

With the second group, "I need a volunteer" was met with a variety of expressions ranging from utter disgust to beady-eyed stare downs challenging me to dare pick them. Others had looks of total disengagement and degrees of boredom approaching imminent death. And there was no discernable movement in the room.

Now, with the adult class. "I need a volunteer." Somewhere and some time along this journey called life, adults have learned that the best way to remain invisible is to avoid eye contact. They immediately became fixated with something on their desk, floor, or sweater. It could have been a speck of dust, but they weren't about to look up until some other poor soul, presumably one less experienced in the ways of survival, was picked. As soon as that individual was picked, the speck of dust had magically vanished, and a look of interest and engagement prevailed.

I was amazed at the contrast. What happens to that child within us full of life, totally spontaneous, willing to enjoy and experience life at every opportunity? Does that child still live inside us, and if so, does it want to come out? How about our families, loved ones, and co-workers? Would they like to experience that part of our personality that has lain dormant and has done so possibly since kindergarten? What is it we are so afraid of, and why do we have this obsession with always being safe? And most importantly, how does this obsession with being safe affect our sense of humor? I shared these three experiences with the class and a vigorous discussion pursued.

There was general agreement among the class that it was inappropriate to volunteer for anything, and yet the class could not come up with one example when volunteering for something turned out to have negative consequences. On the other hand, there were several examples cited when volunteering turned out to have a very positive effect. The examples included a great date and hopefully an upcoming engagement as a result of volunteering to fill sand bags for flood victims. Another student received recognition and a spot on the evening news as a result of volunteer work at a nursing home in addition to part-time work. There were a variety of other examples, and the warning to avoid volunteering seems to have its basis in the military; however, no one was able to cite specifically how that originated.

There was also agreement that the parents had considerable influence in the atmosphere that exists in the home, and their behaviors set the mood and many of the beliefs that influence behaviors later in life. These behaviors may be as subtle as establishing the mood that exists at breakfast or whether the family even met for organized meals. Traditions around holidays are established by the parents in addition to a variety of accepted behaviors including language, allowance, snacks, bedtimes, phone usage, homework, friends, household chores, and the list goes on. All of this would have considerable influence on one's disposition or in context with our discussion, one's sense of humor.

"Dr. Haviland, it seems as if we all are in agreement that parents and the home environment are critical players in the development of this sixth sense. (We had come to an agreement that we would refer to this trait as a sense to facilitate conversation), but it also appears obvious that somewhere along the line the individual begins to establish beliefs and behaviors that are independent of his or her parents, and the uniqueness of the individual personality begins."

"Thank you, Glenn, very well stated. Let's take a look. The other characteristic that seems to jump out is our desire to be safe, avoid risk, and conform in order to fit in. Why is that so important to us as individuals? As young children, we seem to be totally oblivious to this need. We run about totally spontaneously and creative in every aspect, and yet as adults we are almost zombie-like in our behaviors, why?

"Yes sir, your name, please?"

"Gary Reynolds."

"Welcome, Gary. Let's hear what you have to say," I encouraged.

"I think the whole thing has to do with self-confidence. If we lack confidence, the last thing we want to do is venture out into the spotlight and take a risk that may result in our embarrassment."

"That makes sense. Therefore, when opportunity presents itself, we have a

tendency, as a rule, to take the safe, secure, and more predictable route. Is that what you're saying?" I questioned.

"Right on," was his immediate response.

"Can you give me an example of that in your own life? I urged.

"How many do you want?" he asked.

"Give us one to work with would be fine. Perhaps a recent one."

"How does last week sound?" he needled.

"Go for it," I encouraged.

"Okay, I'll try to give you the condensed version," he volunteered.

*"It all began my senior year in high school. We were playing our arch rival in football, and I managed to catch a pass while running out of bounds, hit the Gatorade table, and knocked over three of the opponents' cheerleaders in the process. When I saw it on tape, it looked rather impressive. But the real fireworks started when I looked up, and just like in the movies, time stood still as I was looking into the bluest eyes I'd ever seen. (*Moans from the class). *Hold on, it gets better,"* he warned us.

"I found out her name was Sylvia, and I had a picture of her from the football program, with cheerleaders included, hanging on my wall until last weekend, which is almost four years after the sideline crash. She came with her husband of three months to my cousin's wedding last week, and we physically met at the open bar. She said she remembered the high school incident vividly and had always hoped that I would give her a call for a Coke, a date, or anything in between," Gary continued in dramatic fashion, much to the enjoyment of the class.

"I'm not even sure how I responded to her, but I do remember a whole sequence of flashbacks as I reflected on how many times I had thought about making that bold call to her and never did. And now never will." Silence in the classroom.

"Dr. Haviland, I consider myself to be a confident kind of guy. Why do you think I didn't have the courage to make that call?"

Section VII

Critical Choices

The previous question presented an opportunity that I had anticipated would occur sometime during this discussion; it has to do with one's apparent willingness to take risks in order to be the person we want to be. I had been exposed to the theory years before while working as a probation officer and later teaching criminal justice at Northern Michigan University in Marquette, Michigan. The foundation of the theory is found in the second half of a book entitled *The Psychology of Self-esteem* by Nathaniel Branden. I took liberties with his theories in order to outline it on the board for the current students and keep it in context with our discussion relating to humor. I presented the concept to the students.

I suspect Branden's down and dirty response to Gary's question, *"Why do you think I didn't make that call?"* would be *"Because you felt unworthy."* Branden would then go on to explain that underlying one's desire for security and safety is a deep seated feeling of being unworthy and incompetent.

Preceding the above mental sequence is a mental foundation that is rooted in emotion opposed to intellect. The below sequence is a precursor to the above progression beginning with a feeling of incompetence. The entire sequence of response and development exist in order to remain safe and secure and avoid challenge and risk.

The entire progression from the initial stimulation at the bottom to the immobilization at the top due to the desire for security looks something like this:

I was interrupted at this point by Gary. *"It's amazing how much are desire to remain safe influences all that we do and say."*

"Well, stay with me," I encouraged, *"because when you see the option that was available to you it may make more sense. Branden would suggest there is another option (positive) that was also available to you given the identical circumstances. Bear in mind, this progression in both thinking and behavior appears to be spontaneous in any given situation; however in truth, the beliefs that govern the behaviors are well entrenched in the fiber of the personality and continually reinforced on a daily basis. In short, people who know you well can pretty much anticipate and predict your behavior in most circumstances."*

NEGATIVE	↑	**POSITIVE**
Security		Risk
Safe		Challenge
Unworthy		Worthy
Incompetent		Competent
Lacks Confidence		Self Confident
Out of Control		In Control
Emotion		Intellect
Reactive		Active

Every decision is not a decision of **What to do**, but a decision of **Who you are!**

"The suggestion is, if one has progressed in one's development, keeping in mind the influences of the home environment, parents, peer group, and society in general along the positive vertical, perhaps that decision to ask Sylvia out would not have been so difficult," I offered.

Notice each undesirable trait (on the left) has a corresponding desirable trait on the right. As one progresses up the left scale they accumulate considerable baggage. Repeated daily and over a sequence of years, it is easy to understand how individual personalities become so apparent or obvious to others.

"I had no idea that much thought went into the decision," Gary confessed.

"That's the irony. According to my understanding of Branden's work, the truth is probably very little thought went into your decision. You had a lifetime, in this instance probably sixteen or seventeen years, of being programmed to seek safety, security, and conformity since kindergarten. Therefore, in most situations, the less risky way is usually the chosen way. Bear in mind, the catalyst for this decision is emotion, not intellect. This explanation goes a long way in explaining why it is that so many people end up living a life that is far less than what they imagined. They have a lifetime history of responding emotionally rather than intellectually to a variety of different opportunities in order to be safe, (and avoid risk); therefore they gain the security they desire.

Unfortunately, there are consequences that accompany this reaction. People end up marrying people they are not compatible with, stay in dead-end careers, have unwanted children, and the list goes on, in an effort to seek safety and security."

"Why would having children provide safety and security?" Jennifer asked.

I clarified the statement. *"I shouldn't have included that in the example. I think that applies more to the conformity or predictability that exist at a particular stage of life in order to fit in."*

"The way you explain it, or this guy Branden explains it, we have very little control over our lives because we have been programmed to respond a certain way, and for the most part an emotional way in most circumstances," Jason offered in a rather defeatist tone.

"Quite the contrary," I responded.

"Branden implies we are what we are as a result of the influences and experiences we have had. However, we have a choice as to where we go from here and therefore what we become and consequently, the life that we live," I went on to explain.

Most people look at life as a never-ending bombardment of situations that require decisions that must be made, and as we have discussed, for the most part respond emotionally in order to be safe and secure. Another way of stating the obvious is to do or choose to do what is necessary in order to avoid risk or change. There is a variety of research that addresses why people avoid risk and change. At the top of the list is that change involves uncertainty, and we are right back to our innate desire to remain safe. Change also provides an opportunity to fail, and to one who feels incompetent, the prospect of change borders on a death wish.

Another interesting dynamic in addition to the fear of failure that accompanies change is the fear of success which may be equally immobilizing. Imagine the guilt, the alienation, increased expectations, and loss of identity that success creates in one who feels unworthy. This observation goes a long way in explaining what appears to be the blatant course of self-destruction so many "overnight successes" seem to pursue. It is very difficult to be someone you feel unworthy to be.

Branden says rather than this never-ending succession of complex situations and decision-making, most situations may be reduced to one of three choices, which he refers to as volitions. In a given situation, we choose to:

In reality, these three dynamics frequently overlap:

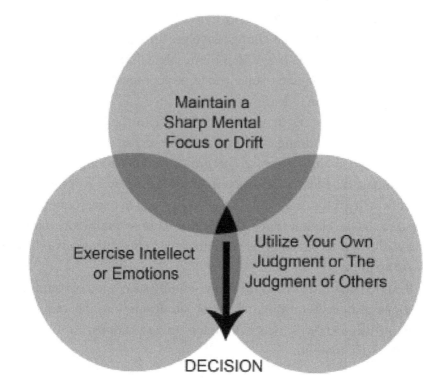

In essence, life is a series of situations, each of which requires a response. That response may be based on maintaining a sharp mental focus, exercising one's intellect, and utilizing one's own judgment, or one may drift, rely on emotional responses, and trust the judgment of others. Any given situation may be a combination of all three options or any one option.

"What would be an example of what you're talking about?" Reid asked.

"Well, let me ask, what will you do when this class ends tonight at 9:30, Reid?"

"I usually stop at the sports bar and watch the end of the Monday night game," he offered.

"And, what time will you get home?" I inquired.

"About midnight, maybe 12:30 was his response.

The class chuckled, anticipating what was coming next. *"Long game?"* I questioned.

"Well, we have to diagnose and critique the game, ya know," explained Reid. More snickering from the class.

"What do you think Branden would say," I asked.

"Well, I'm guessing this guy Branden wouldn't be a big fan of football. Therefore, he would probably say I was existing in mental drift, being led by emotions and trusting the judgment or the influence of others over my own," was his response.

"I'm not sure, but out of curiosity, what are some of the rest of you doing after class that Branden might look on more favorably? I asked.

Some of the responses: *"I go to work." "I have a guitar lesson." "I meet with a study group,"* and a variety of other responses that would be recorded on the positive side of the equation were offered.

"Wow, I'm starting to feel guilty. Is there ever any time to just kick back and relax? Reid asked.

"I would suspect that Branden would be very supportive of a relaxation break when appropriate, but I suspect most of us justify frequent and very long extended breaks with little regard for the time wasted, and more importantly, the opportunity to do something more constructive with our time. Now the more critical question may be how many of these extended breaks can one take before beginning to feel unworthy?"

There seems to be a great deal of consistency between what Branden is suggesting and the development of one's self-esteem.

"Before we take a break, let's briefly circle back and tie this discussion relating to self-esteem back to an individual's humorous disposition. Any takers? Gary, I believe you were responsible for taking us on this ride. Any summary thoughts?" I urged.

"Sure. For openers, it seems like it would be totally inconsistent to think that an individual who possesses this desirable trait of humor could be one who feels out of control and lacks confidence. It appears that this desirable humorous disposition would develop if one consistently followed the course of positive choices, and probably impossible to achieve if one constantly followed one's emotional instinct," he offered.

"Wow, pretty heavy stuff, Gary. You sure you want to stick with it?" I asked.

"Yea, I'm going to stick with it. And to think all I wanted was a date," he inserted.

And I jokingly responded, *"Isn't there anyone who will go out with Gary?"*

Much to my surprise, from the back of the room a very attractive coed responded, *"I will."*

To which Gary responded, *"Are you for real?"*

And she responded, *"Sure, I'll give it a shot. I'm always good for a Starbuck's date."*

"You are on, my friend," Gary responded, and the class let out a huge cheer as we dismissed for break. It was a most interesting night.

When we returned from break, I resumed with the following, *"Over the break, I had an opportunity to meet with both Stephanie and Gary to be sure they didn't feel any pressure to commit to the Starbuck's date. For your information, both are fine with the commitment and plan to attend. However, this does present a teachable moment. Let's examine what just happened in context with our discussion of this evening.*

First of all, neither Gary nor Stephanie knows anyone else in the class. Why would that be important?" I asked.

"I know," was an enthusiastic response from Brittany. *"When Gary put out the invitation, Stephanie accepted the offer, and then when Gary reciprocated, it would appear both had left themselves very vulnerable for rejection. However, because neither of them knows anyone in the class, the influence of a peer group was minimized. What do you think?"* she proudly announced.

"I think you're right on target," I responded. *"Let's talk about the choices involved that would affect self-esteem."* I urged. *"Stephanie, if you wouldn't mind?"* I invited.

"Go for it," she responded.

"Do you feel like you were maintaining a sharp mental focus during that exchange or drifting? Was my first question directed to Stephanie.

She responded, *"Totally focused. I completely identified with his lost opportunity with Sylvia, as most of us probably do, but as I listened to him, I was thinking maybe she missed out on a pretty good opportunity."*

"How about the other two dynamics? Were you exercising intellect or emotions and trusting your judgment or that of others?" I inquired.

"That's easy. Let me answer the second part first. Because I don't know another person in this room, the judgment was totally mine. And was it intellect or emotion? Perhaps some of each. From an intellectual standpoint, the truth is, I'm not asking the guy to marry me, I am just having a cup of coffee, I will meet him there, and I will have an escape plan, perhaps an expected call from home which I can't miss, to be utilized if necessary. And the emotional part, I like his dimples." Laughter erupted.

"And now for the Cash Cab question, what effect did that exchange have on their individual self-esteem and by inference, their humorous disposition?"

Unanimous agreement, *"Both would be enhanced."*

Rick Myers generated a new round of discussion by asking," *Wow, when you isolate a particular example like Gary and Stephanie, it seems pretty obvious how their spontaneous willingness to take a risk is consistent with building confidence, but what would have happened if one of them would have said 'no thanks' to the date?"*

"I don't know. What do you think, class?" I queried.

Marti offered, *"Wouldn't it depend on how secure their confidence or self-esteem is at this point in life?"*

"And what would determine that, Marti?" I asked.

"The experiences they had earlier in life that served to either reinforce a positive disposition or reinforce a negative disposition, according to what we said earlier," she responded.

"And if you had to guess, what would you guess their early experience would be, for the most part?" I asked.

"I would guess they had been positive *for the most part,"* she volunteered.

"Why do you say that?" I asked.

"Because if their early experiences had been predominantly negative, they probably wouldn't have been so willing to risk rejection so publicly at this point of their lives."

Rick Myers jumped back in, *"Yea, but he may turn out to be Jack-the-Ripper."*

Strong head nods of support from the class.

"And that is precisely the type of mental argument that a more cautious person would entertain to justify not doing it and remaining safe. I suspect we could list two thousand reasons why Stephanie shouldn't do it, and they will

range from every vampire movie, to Saw I, II, III and everything in between, to the brokendown car he may own to the possibility that he smokes and she doesn't. Any of these possibilities may serve as a good reason not to do it. For most people, there just needs to be one, one reason not to go, in order to justify remaining safe," I offered.

"And Branden is suggesting these parameters were set long ago; therefore, the possibility of even considering going is totally remote to a large segment of the population," Kim accurately clarified. *"But the reality is Gary may be 'The One' for Stephanie, and if she doesn't go, she will never know."*

Glenn Wright came to life, *"Please help me. I'm exhausted. How many of these decisions do you think the average person would have to make in a lifetime, thousands, millions?"*

"At one time I would have thought thousands during a lifetime, but I think this is part of Branden's message. We think we are these super complex beings in our thinking; however, the truth of the matter is we are so channeled in our mode of response, most decisions are already made internally, (or intuitively), prior to the situation occurring. Therefore, there really is no decision to be made. Furthermore, the people we associate with have a tendency to know what our response will be before they ask the question."

"The difficult or awkward situation occurs when we don't know how another will answer. If I may reflect back on our two dating examples, what really prevented Gary from asking Sylvia out back in high school?" I asked.

"Because he didn't know her, he didn't know how she would respond; therefore, he played it safe and didn't ask," Jason offered boldly.

"Exactly," I offered. *"How does that differ with what happened with Stephanie tonight? Jason, would you care to handle that?"*

"Well, first of all, he didn't really ask her. You asked if anyone was willing to go out with Gary. And when Stephanie answered 'yes' so quickly, Gary really didn't have the opportunity to think about it; he spontaneously agreed," Jason proudly stated.

"I'll accept that. Just reflect on the number of times you have initially wanted to do something, but you've overthought it and convinced yourself it may not be the 'safest' or most 'secure' choice; therefore, you had better not do it. This becomes the lament of older people when they reflect on lives that have proven to be less than fulfilling, 'If only I had'…"

"Before I forget, let me comment on the 'complex life' we think we live. I remember reading about the frequency of these 'emotional moments' we have during a lifetime. As I recall, the author cited, on average we have ten defining moments, seven critical choices and five pivotal people that have considerable influence on our lives. He goes on to say what appears to be a life of variety is frequently the same or similar experience being repeated. For example, if you dated but remained with that person due to a fear that you may not have anyone, has that really been a challenging experience or has that been a desire to remain secure? Now apply that same reason to the job you have and don't like but remain in it. Or consider the risk of going on vacation to add variety to life. Is it really that challenging if you go back to the same place repeatedly or is it again a desire to be safe? Something to think about until we meet again. Class dismissed."

As I sat in my study preparing for next week's class I continued to look at the abbreviated diagram of what we discussed in class the previous week. For convenience sake and to facilitate discussion within the class, we now refer to these three choices that are so instrumental in influencing one's self-esteem and ultimately humorous disposition as CB's or **"Critical Behaviors."** The progressions, positive or negative, that result from these critical behaviors are simply referred to as **"Consequences."**

Critical Behaviors

Positive: Focus/Intellect/Own Judgment
Active/Intellect/In-Control/Self-Confident/Competent/Worthy/
Challenge/Risk

****

Negative: Drift/Emotions/Judgment of Others
Reactive/Emotion/Out-of-Control/Lacks Confidence/Incompetent/
Unworthy/Safe/Security

Could it possibly be that simple? In many respects, it seems to be. Most of us can pinpoint those positive defining moments, critical choices, and pivotal people who have contributed to who we are. We can also identify those negative influences that have had a detrimental effect and have not assisted us in becoming the person we want to be. My experience has been that many people can isolate the exact date, time, and emotion that accompanied these influential events.

Unfortunately, the fact that one can identify these specific negative moments frequently provides one with an excuse or justification to continue in a less than desirable state. Therefore, we have a tendency to be reactive in nature, speaking and acting as if we have little control over these outside influences and subsequently view ourselves as unworthy. The older and more educated we become merely provides more experiences to support current behaviors, and we learn to articulate these excuses in a more convincing fashion.

I received a heavy dose of this helpless victim status as a probation worker and also later as I worked and taught in the field of criminal justice. I found very few individuals who had been convicted of crimes ranging from shoplifting to murder who felt any remorse or responsibility for their actions. And most were extremely articulate in identifying the outside influence that precipitated their actions. Perhaps Charles Sykes, author of A *Nation of Victims* said it best, "The chorus of powerlessness over one's problems has become so shrill that if Walt Whitman were to come back to America in the 20th century, he wouldn't hear America singing. He would hear America whining."

SECTION VIII

Emotional Tones

During my doctoral studies relating to criminal justice and higher education, I came across a fascinating work by Ruth Minshull. In summary, it answered the question of how predictable people become in revealing their disposition, and they do it via one common denominator, emotion. Briefly stated, individuals manifest one of fifteen emotional tones, much like the easily identified tones in music. These emotional tones range from grim to great. According to Minshull, "Once we know the basic characteristics of each emotion, we can meet a person for the first time and, within minutes; we can understand his present frame of mind."

This intriguing concept became fascinating to me when reading the book, *Helter Skelter* which is the accounting of the Charles Manson murders. Manson has always been an enigma to those who work in the criminal justice field, not so much due to the celebrity of the victims but to the eagerness of the perpetrators to willingly kill at the direction of another person, Charles Manson.

In Part III of *Helter Skelter*, it implies that Manson was privy to the same knowledge base that Ruth Minshull later documented in her book entitled; *How To Choose Your People*. I found this connection to be captivating. If Minshull is correct, one well versed in recognizing the emotional tone of another may match that tone in order to befriend that person and subsequently rise above that tone in order to manipulate all tones below. As Minshull states it, "We will then know how well he's surviving and whether he will be an asset or a liability in our relationship." I would share this epiphany at the next class session, and the following exchange unfolded.

"Dr. Haviland, let me see if I'm keeping up with this conversation. You're saying that the one thing people have in common is emotion, and each of us gives off an emotional vibe that others pick up on, and if properly trained, one may become very sensitive to that tone, and if desired, may match that tone in order to develop a relationship?

In George Langelett's book, *How Do I Keep My Employees Motivated (2014)*, he refers to this as empathy-based management and defines it as real communication that occurs when we listen with understanding and respond in a way that honors the unique experience of others.

And this tone is most likely reflective of one's disposition, which we also associate with the trait of humor? Am I close?

"You, Mike Ridgeway, are dead on." I applauded his insight. *"I might add that is not as strange as it sounds, nor was Minshull the first to suggest such a phenomena. Some people attribute the same ability to animals, which explains a dog's overt reaction to some strangers but not others. Many of the horse whisperers and veterinarian types have been associated with a positive vibe that animals may sense."*

"Dr. and Natalie Zunin entitled their book, Contact, The First Four Minutes, claiming four minutes is the average time, demonstrated by careful observation, during which strangers in a social situation interact before they decide to part or continue their encounter," I continued. *"We can go way back to the pioneers in effective communication and find evidence of the same. Napoleon Hill is his seminal work, Law of Success, proclaimed the same type of personal connection was due to the vibration of bodily fluids that encompass all atomic matter. It sounds pretty sophisticated, but really it is another way of explaining why it is that when you can walk into a room of strangers you frequently get a sense of whose company you will enjoy and whom you would like to avoid. Where's that coming from?"*

"Now the question becomes how valuable would that make you, if in fact people, felt that positive attraction emitting from you? Or in the parlance of 'business speak,' what would that make you worth to a company? I think we are starting to sense why this mysterious trait of a humorous disposition is so valuable," I offered.

"It reminds me of the credit card ad, 'It's priceless," offered Reid.

"Excuse me, Dr. Haviland, but a few of us were talking at break and came to the conclusion that it couldn't be this easy," stated newcomer Leroy.

"Elaborate for me, Leroy. What are we talking about, and what is so easy?" I requested.

"Well, if I understand this correctly, now that most of us are free from our parental, and for the most part our peer group influence, whether that be positive or negative, we are free to exercise our own CB's and make mentally sharp, intellectual choices independent of the judgments of others and create this

humorous disposition that will be welcomed by all. Does that pretty much cover it?" He asked.

"First let me ask how thick your skin is? Or may I use this as a teaching moment?" I asked.

"It's as thick as an alligator, go for it," he urged.

"There are two issues here. First, Minshull would point out that emotional tones like to group with others of a like tone. Therefore, I assume those of you who were discussing the unlikelihood that it could all be that easy were in agreement?" I asked.

"That's true," he agreed.

"Can you see how awkward it would be for a classmate emitting a different tone to join in on the conversation? For instance, if someone were to approach the group with a very enthusiastic; 'Isn't this great to know how easy it is to take control of our lives?' I would assume they might receive a rather cool reception from your group?"

"Yea, I would say so," he agreed.

"Can you imagine another group in addition to your group, meeting in the same room during the same break?" I asked.

"Yes, I can. Okay, I get it. That would be an example of individuals seeking out a group emitting an alternative tone, a tone totally different than the tone of our group?"

"Precisely," I responded. Now let's take a look at the tone of your group. Given your limited knowledge of Minshull's tones and the specific labels she attached to her tones, how would you describe the tone of your group overall?" I asked.

"Well, I would say that we are skeptical and have a hard time believing one can take control of their life that easily," he offered.

I responded, *"At what point did I, speaking on behalf of Brandon and Minshull, ever indicate that it would be easy?"*

"In retrospect, I don't think you did. I think the concepts make it sound easy," was his response.

I agreed, *"That's fair, but let's take a closer look at the tone that prevailed within your group at break. You indicated you were 'skeptical.' Do any other words come to mind, or if I pushed for an answer, do you really think people can change their disposition by merely changing their CB's?" I* urged.

His response, *"If you pushed for an answer, as much as I would like to believe, I would have to say no. Does that mean I flunk the class?"* We all had a good laugh, and I could understand their doubts. If it is that easy, why don't more people do it?

I picked up Minshull's book and began to read, *"Let's consult the source. From my reading I think I recognize the category or tone. Let me read and paraphrase excerpts from the text and you tell me if it captures the overall mood of the group."*

"This tone wants to hang on to the past and does not want to attach to new concepts, because if they do, it rids them of the opportunity to whine. Sometimes people group together on this tone, crying for sympathy and help while offering nothing in return. No solution, no contribution, no concession is ever enough." I continued, *"If you suggest a solution to one existing in this tone, she will dissolve in a puddle and tell you it's impossible. She doesn't expect to rid herself of the problem; she merely wanted to wallow in the horribleness of it all ... and she wanted company. No person of this tone accepts a simple solution, and one firmly entrenched in this tone doesn't accept any solution.* I questioned, *"Shall I continue?"*

"No thanks. I now realize my skin is not that thick, and I'm disbanding the group that met at break." We all laughed.

"Leroy, don't be too hard on you because Minshull warns us not to judge too quickly. A person may demonstrate a specific lower tone; however, their existence in that tone may be only temporary and strongly influenced by a variety of circumstances that are affecting that person at that time. However, before I provide everyone a convenient excuse for existing in a lower tone, Minshull cautions us to not be too forgiving, because if in fact a person has chosen to live in this lower tone, you as a higher-toned individual have one of three choices; either merge with this lower tone in order to fit in, or flee from their influence out of self-preservation or temporarily match their tone in anticipation of bringing them up scale."

I added an additional caution to that, *"Unfortunately, this is a trap too many people fall into. In their effort to assist another to come up on the tone scale (frequently referred to as an enabler), they sacrifice their own lives. This is the person who looks back and asks, 'Where did I go wrong?' or 'If I could only do it all over again.'"*

"These group dynamics are fascinating. Let me give another example. We are

all familiar with gossip, and most of us could label the individual going back as far as middle school who was the instigator of many of the rumors that circulated among our classmates. As we progress in life and enter different social settings whether it is high school, college, work, church or social groups of any type, we again can identify the person who assumes that role. However, in order for gossip or rumors to have wings, it must have an audience. The world is full of people who don't consider themselves to be 'gossips' but merely spectators listening to the gossip, and admittedly may pass along what they heard but only to their close friends. These individuals would be shocked and hurt if they were ever identified or included in the category of 'gossips.' Can you see the irony of this?" I asked.

"At the risk of going down another rat hole, I should mention in addition to Minshull warning us of this self-deception, Branden also tells us to take notice of this personality flaw. Branden refers to it as pseudo self-esteem; I refer to it as the imposter phenomenon. According to Branden, 'So intensely does a man feel the need of a positive view of himself, that he may evade, repress, distort his judgment, disintegrate his mind-in order to avoid coming face to face with facts that would affect his self-appraisal adversely. If and to the extent that men lack self-esteem, they feel driven to fake it.'"

I added, *"One can only wonder if this dynamic was at play when we evaluated our own sense of humor at an average of 7.5, and yet our boss or supervisor averaged 4.0. How humbling would it be if we asked our subordinates to evaluate us?"*

"Before we move on, I would like to elaborate on one other point that Leroy made which I agree with," I offered, and Leroy inserted, *"Please continue,"* which got a good chuckle from the class.

"It has to do with his observation that this concept of Branden's makes it too easy for one to gain control of one's life, and I would like to briefly address this based on an experience I had while living in Australia. This seemed like too good an opportunity to pass up an example of something both easy and beneficial to us, and yet we don't necessarily pursue it. *"I owned a health spa in Australia and spent a good portion of the day soliciting new memberships. Well, let me ask the relevant question to the class." "Please, by a show of hands, how many of you would like to be in better physical condition?"* Virtually every hand in the classroom went up. *"That's*

what I would have anticipated. Now the next question, who in here doesn't know how to do that?" Not a hand in the air.

"And that, my friends, is the point to be made. We all know, and every prospect that walked into my spa knew, and knew from a very young age, it boils down to exercise and diet. No tricks, no gimmicks. It's just that simple. And yet, we live in an obese nation, with very few people unaware of what is necessary to get their bodies in the shape they desire. Now mind you, I'm not saying it will be easy, but it is necessary. Neither Branden nor Minshull said it would be easy, just necessary to make the appropriate choices. Instead, we invest in billions of dollars annually in pills and devices advertised on late night television hoping there will be some miracle drug, apparatus, or short cut that will enable us to avoid the obvious."

"Now please put this in context with our discussions relating back to a humorous disposition because the same principle applies. Humor is a trait that is extremely desirable, lucrative, and beneficial to us in both a personal and professional capacity. We know it is achievable if we make the right decisions, and yet few of us choose to. Therein lies why we admire and reward the few who have made the necessary sacrifice and truly possess this trait of humor. Let's take a break."

Following break, we began examining what gives a humorous disposition value.

"Dr. Haviland, right before break you were talking about how rare it is that one has a humorous disposition in spite of the fact the formula for achieving this disposition is relatively simple. Is the fact that it is so rare that makes it so valuable? I mean is it like the value of a rare painting?"

"That's part of it, Ted. If we just took the position that there are few people who really possess this trait that would probably make them more valuable than the rest of us. Aside from just being rare, what other characteristics does the trait suggest would exist, and why would that be valuable to an organization?" I asked.

Kim was first to respond. *"If we assume they have developed this disposition in conjunction with the appropriate CB's, there are a variety of good things that would emerge by definition."* I encouraged her to continue, *"For instance?"*

"Because of their confidence and willingness to accept challenges and take risk, I think they would create an exciting work atmosphere," she offered.

"Do you think this is the kind of atmosphere or boss that you would like to work for?" I asked.

"Absolutely," was her immediate response.

"As a rule, do you think this type of boss would be moody?" I inquired.

"I wouldn't think so," she volunteered

I immediately inserted, *"Perhaps this is what makes these people so valuable is the fact they are so predictable. Due to their confidence and willingness to take risk, they are approachable and receptive to people and their ideas, because they are not threatened. Now Ted, I'm coming back at you. What I'm suggesting is that trait that makes art so valuable, in addition to being rare, is the fact that people recognize it and therefore there is an element of comfort, similar to that of seeing a familiar face, opposed to seeing a stranger."*

"In some respects, the predictable and receptive nature of these people possessing a humorous disposition makes them approachable," I concluded. I couldn't help but have a flashback to an article I was reading last night. *Fortune* magazine selected Steve Jobs as the "CEO of the Decade." One of the articles interviewed eight people who rarely speak publicly about Jobs. In an interview with Andrea Jung, Chairman and CEO of Avon and who sits on the Apple board, she states, *"There's an extraordinary openness in the boardroom. Any board member would feel free to challenge an idea or raise a concern. It's not only been gratifying; it's been great."* The article also addresses the simplicity of his approach, *"He (Jobs) makes it sound so simple, but he's taking on things that are extraordinarily complex and risky. He's laser-focused on getting it right."* Another reference to Jobs and consistent with our discussion relating to tones was made by journalist Michael Moritz, *"Steve's got a fabulous eye and a terrific ear. Most people in Silicon Valley or in the consumer electronics business are tone deaf, off-key. Steve has perfect pitch."* I'm sure Minshull would appreciate that metaphor.

"We can assume the opposite would be true?" asked Marti.

"Elaborate, please," I encouraged.

"Well, the person who does not possess this temperament would be one who is lacking in confidence, therefore struggling with feelings of incompetency, therefore seeking the safe and secure route, I would assume," she offered.

I challenged, *"What do you think their primary trait or characteristic would be in contrast to the predictable boss we just described?*

"I would assume they would be somewhat defensive and not very receptive to new ideas or risk," was her response.

I opened up to the class, *"Anyone ever had a boss like that?"* Virtually every hand in the class went up. *"Aha, a teachable moment. That explains two isolated facts we have addressed earlier. First, it explains why our bosses scored so low on our earlier survey rating them on a one-to-ten scale, and secondly, why people that possess the humorous disposition are so valuable to an organization. Because they are receptive to others and their ideas, they are capable of diffusing conflict before it dominates the organization."*

"Dr. Haviland, before we get going, could I share an experience I had this weekend that is textbook perfect for what we've been talking about?" This request was made by Jason who hadn't said much during the semester but seemed to be taking it all in.

I responded, *"Under one condition."* Does this have the potential to take us down another rat hole and dominate the discussion for the rest of the evening?" I asked.

"Yes, it has that potential," was his response, while the class cheered.

"Well, if that's the case, go for it!" I encouraged.

"To begin, I've been fascinated with these emotional tones we've been talking about, and I had the opportunity to see them in action this weekend. My uncle Bill won five tickets to the Vikings game on Sunday so he invited his three brothers and me. I'm sure my invitation was influenced by the fact I drive an SUV and willingly volunteered as the designated driver, which I was fine with.

"I picked Uncle Bill up first which allowed us a good thirty-five minutes prior to our next stop. Bill is a great guy, is doing very well as owner of his own business, and the Viking tickets were in recognition of a state sales contest which he had won. He was asking how graduate school was going for me, and we had a good conversation. I was telling him about this class and specifically about the emotional tones, which he thoroughly enjoyed. What struck me was how the mood and conversation changed as soon as my uncle Sid got in the car, and I think, because I had just been talking about the tones, it really caught my attention how the atmosphere within the car changed as we picked up each additional passenger. I began to listen very carefully to the contribution of each passenger during the

four hour drive, and it was unreal how consistent they were in expressing a given tone regardless of the topic. The difference in tones was amazing given they were all raised in the same home environment."

"*I think Ruth Minshull would be pleased with your observation,*" I encouraged him.

He continued, "*Now here's the big question. If I give you examples of their contributions to the conversation, will you be able to tell me their emotional tone?*"

"*I'm sure Ruth would warn me not to bite on this with such limited exposure, but she's not here, so let's go for it. Allow me to get my resources in order.*" I removed her book, *How to Choose Your People,* from my briefcase. Jason removed his notes he had scribbled during the commute to the Vikings game.

"*Great,*" he said. "*I made note of what they said regarding five different topics during the day in order to compare.*"

"*Wow, I sense we are at the entrance of a giant rat hole at this moment,*" I said. However, I wanted to continue due to his obvious enthusiasm and copious notes, not to mention this was his initial contribution to the class.

"*Fire when ready,*" I commanded. "*No wait, let me set up a grid. You said there were four passengers in addition to yourself and you addressed four different topics. Is that correct?*" I asked.

"*Yes, that is correct.*" I drew a 4 X 6 grid allowing for the four participants, their four responses and a place to identify the tone, if possible. Down the side I listed the uncles by name: Bill, Phil, Dick, and Sid. "*And the topics?*" I requested.

"*I recorded their individual tone on four occasions: When they entered the car, opinion of the Vikings team, stopping at a rest stop, and when they were dropped off after the game,*" Jason volunteered.

We then began to fill in the chart according to what each uncle volunteered, and midway through the exercise as each uncle's emotional tone became obvious, students were yelling out in anticipation of what each uncle would contribute. The contributions from the class members, not privy to the conversation that took place during the drive, were amazingly consistent with what Jason had to offer. This proved to be a valuable teaching point regarding the consistency and predictability of a response once a tone is established.

We concluded the exercise by labeling the tone manifested along with some of the characteristics consistent with that tone. The completed chart:

Trip to Vikings Game

Tone Scale	Characteristics of tone	Entering the car	The Vikings	Rest Stop	Departure
3.5 Interest Uncle Bill	Maintains interest and involvement. Inspires others/ Contagious	Ready to go. Concerned about me	"We are lucky to be seeing such a good team."	"That will be refreshing."	"Thanks so much for the game. Have a great week."
2.0 Antagonism Uncle Phil	Chip on the shoulder. Challenges & disagrees.	"How come you didn't pick me up first?"	"What's so great about winning a soft schedule?"	"If we stop it will just make us late. I say drive on."	"I expected a lot more. It wasn't one of their better games."
2.0 Fear Uncle Dick	Everything is dangerous. Postpones living.	Dressed for survival. "Be careful of deer, a good friend of his just ..."	"If anything happens to Peterson the Vikings are done for the year."	"Is that the same rest stop where the girl was raped and kidnapped? I don't think she was ever found."	"Let me get my keys out first. You never know what can happen. A friend of mine..."
0.5 Grief Uncle Sid	Whiner/victim clings to the past. Seeks pity, dependent. No simple solutions.	"I would have been ready, but my wife never..."	"They're just not like the 'Vikes' of '82"	"Try to park close so we don't have to walk."	"Great, home just in time to fold laundry."

This example also explains why we approach certain individuals given a specific topic and avoid others given the same topic. Although we may not have referred to them as emotional tones in the past, our subconscious mind has categorized them as such and we act accordingly to the best of our abilities.

A good example of this is evident in discussions relating to politics. We may never have had discussions with a peer regarding their political persuasion; however, we suspect what their views will be and offer opinions that we anticipate will be consistent with theirs in order to avoid conflict. When they blatantly demonstrate their party allegiance, we immediately make assumptions on how they will respond on a variety of issues.

My guess is most people consider themselves to be independent thinkers, and I am sure Branden would suggest this is in order to maintain a positive self-esteem; however, the pressure to conform to a "party line or position" may serve to influence one to a far greater degree than one would care to admit. This is never more evident than in Congress when critical issues require a vote. Put this is context with the CB's (critical behaviors) that have been discussed earlier, in particular regarding the importance of utilizing one's own judgment over the judgment of other's (party), and it is easy to empathize with those who hold elected offices and their desire to maintain high self-esteem.

Conflict takes place when one jumps or mixes tones and communication breaks down. By definition, individuals who exist high on the tone scale are individuals who hold themselves in high esteem, and the reverse of this is equally true; it is virtually impossible to have low self-esteem and exist high on the tone scale. We may temporarily be caught off guard when confronted with pseudo self-esteem. This dynamic exists when one does not conform to the perception we hold of them and their behaviors are totally inconsistent with our expectations; we feel we've been duped. We want individuals who hold high office and maintain celebrity status to be self-confident, self-assured, and consistently demonstrating a high tone. Unfortunately, the outer appearance may be in great conflict with the inner being, and we read about it in the headlines on a daily basis.

"Thank you, Jason for that contribution. Is there another rat hole we can crawl down this evening? Oh, wait, before I forget, Minshull also coaches us to be aware of some additional cues in detecting an individual's emotional tone:

1. *How do you feel after talking with them?*
2. *How are they surviving?*
3. *Are they clearly understood?*
4. *What do they talk about?*
5. *Is the conversation shared equally between the two of you?*
6. *What is the frequency of accidents in their life?*
7. *What are they accomplishing?*
8. *How easily do they adjust to other tones?*
9. *What are their ethical standards?*
10. *What role do possessions play in their life?*
11. *Where is their orientation (past, present or future)?*

"Hopefully, at this point in time, you will be able to discern what the desirable answers to the above questions are. If not, we may have a bigger problem. Here's an interesting question. How would Jason's four uncles respond to the eleven questions above given their grief, fear, and antagonistic tone of interest? Now, what's next?"

Todd raised his hand. *"I've got one that has been bothering me since we met last time, and it's about Steve Jobs. I've always been a big fan of Jobs and I know he was responsible for 34,000 employees and increasing shareholder wealth by more than $150 billion dollars, but I never saw this humorous disposition that we have talked about."*

"That's an excellent observation, and I'm surprised that it hasn't come up earlier. At this point, I'm not sure what Jobs' net worth was estimated to be. However, he is frequently seen as this stern and sober guy who maintained celebrity status among employees, customers, analysts, and rivals who scream as if he were a rock star when he walked on stage for a keynote event. So where is this humorous disposition that is so valuable? The truth be known, we are all making the same mistake in our assessment of Mr. Jobs. What is it?"

Jennifer took the bait. *"We're measuring the wrong thing."*

"Please explain," I urged.

"We are trying to project our own values and definitions of success on a person who thinks totally independently. From what I have read, he placed very little value on money, possessions, or celebrity status. I went back and read that article you had mentioned in Fortune magazine that declared him CEO of the Decade, complete with cover photo, the whole works, and yet he was not available to be interviewed for the cover story. Most celebrities would have died for that kind of exposure."

Another mistake is to think a sense of humor is demonstrated by a very outgoing personality, complete with abundant laughs and jokes. And if we think that, we are making the same mistake we mentioned the first night of class, and we now know humor has no relationship to jokes or comedy."

"What did you see in Jobs that would be consistent with a humorous disposition?" I asked.

"Well, with the exception of humor and charisma, it appears that he would have the ten remaining traits associated with leadership and our definition of success we identified the first night. His CB's couldn't be more on target, and that produced a very confident man who didn't shy away from challenge or risk. He didn't do anything to suggest he wanted to play it safe. Because we didn't see the man in public that much, it's more difficult to identify his tone. However, his success would certainly suggest he is high tone. I'm really impressed with his intense focus and how receptive he was to the ideas of others. I also think it's great that he was so dedicated to his family." Jennifer's insights were well received by the class.

"If these people are not motivated by the usual trappings of success, what motivates them?" Glenn asked.

SECTION IX

Flow

The best explanation of what motivates people, if not the trappings of success, I've ever heard of is provided by psychologist Mihaly Csikszentmihalyi. He identifies a state of concentration that he calls "flow." This is a state so focused that it amounts to absolute absorption in an activity. The author states that many people may experience this while reading a great book; for him, it was while playing chess. Flow requires complete concentration to the task at hand, a task that requires utilizing the skills that one has to respond to a challenge that complements the skills at hand.

Recognizing that it is impossible to do justice to this enormous topic in these pages, I emailed Dr. Csikszentmihalyi seeking permission to include in this manuscript the diagram and explanation of *Flow* as presented in his book, *Good Business: Leadership, Flow and the Making of Meaning*. Within three minutes, he responded, "Sure, go ahead." I personally think this type of immediate response and willingness to share the intellectual property that he has worked years to create reflects volumes regarding what kind of a man he is. This type of unselfishness exists only at the very top on the "Tones" scale.

In reviewing his "Flow" diagram, some readers will interpret "Flow" as "Balance" within one's life. Maintaining a proper balance is the critical ingredient or foundation to happiness or contentment. Taking on too many challenges in life without a complementary skill set to accomplish these challenges will create anxiety in life. On the other hand, if one doesn't challenge the skill set they have, they will encounter boredom. Maintaining a balance is the secret, and this is when one experiences "Flow."

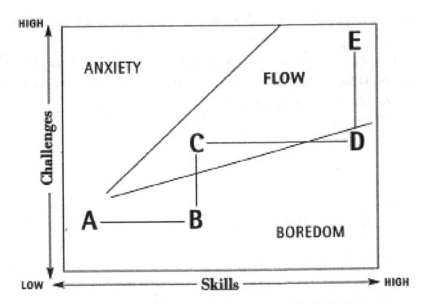

Figure 1: Growth of Complexity Through Flow. The flow experience occurs when both skills and challenges are high. A typical activity starts at A, with low challenges and skills. If one perseveres the skills will increase and the activity becomes boring (B). At that point, one will have to increase the challenges to return to flow (C). This cycle is repeated at higher levels of complexity through D and E. In a good flow activity these cycles can continue almost indefinitely.

In the words of Csikszentmihalyi: "*The ideal balance between challenges and skills never remains stable for long. Either one or the other component predominates, at which point adjustments will be necessary.*" A conclusion that he makes as a result of research and speaking with successful businessmen similar to Steve Jobs: "*Contrary to common perception, there are many successful executives who understand that 'good business' involves more than making money, and who take the responsibility for making their firms an engine for enhancing the quality of life…The quality of the experience is the most important factor affecting overall satisfaction with life.*"

Jason offered a summary statement, "*There seems to be a great deal of consistency for one demonstrating a humorous disposition, a high emotional tone, choosing positive critical behaviors, and now existing in an atmosphere of 'flow'."*

I concurred, *"It certainly appears that way. So now back to our decisive question. What would it be worth for an organization to have an individual at the helm who possesses these traits?"*

SECTION X

Change Avoidance

"*Just before we go there, I have a concern,*" Gary Reynolds admitted. "*Let's just say, I wanted to ask a question for a friend of mind who couldn't be here tonight.*" Laughter from the class.

"*Sure, Gary. What is it your friend wanted to ask?*" I responded.

"*I have discussed what we've been talking about, and he thinks there may be room for him to possibly move up on the tone scale and perhaps develop the kind of confidence necessary for this flow to reveal a humorous disposition so desirable by others and organizations. Any tips you can give me to pass on to him?*" He was smiling now.

"*I think so,*" I responded. "*I'm sorry your friend couldn't make it, but who knows? Perhaps someone in class may benefit from the discussion, which may be long overdue.*"

"*Sounds good to me,*" he said, as the class leaned forward and took out pen and paper.

I began. "*The first step is to do a serious self-evaluation of why you want to change and how you would benefit if in fact you do change. Most people think the response to this is obvious; however, psychotherapists will warn that there are some risks and fears associated with change. Identifying the risk is usually enough to discourage any efforts related to change. Some of the risks or fears we have alluded to before; however, let's briefly identify them once more.*" I listed them on the board:

Risk and Change Avoidance

Involves Uncertainty.

May produce envy from friends

May result in alienation from peers

Presents an opportunity to succeed

Requires action or decision

May cause feelings of guilt

May increase expectations

Inconsistent with self-concept

Opportunity to fail

Coping with failure yields identity

Unworthy

Implies Change

"Change is a very interesting dynamic. I suspect that most people think that they have willingly adjusted to changes in life. However, I would submit that the majority of changes that have taken place in an individual's life are changes that have been necessary for survival, not necessarily improvement, and few have been made voluntarily. And there are good reasons why people don't willingly change. One of the primary reasons we resist change is that change is going to demand something from us, and we are not a generation known for our discipline or making sacrifices. We enjoy the comfort we have, and change introduces the unknown, and the unknown just happens to be one of our greatest fears," I continued.

"If we reflect back to the emotional tones scale, we know that 'fear' is one of the lower tones and frequently serves to immobilize an individual out of fear of what might happen. From a self-esteem perspective, to continue in a negative state may not necessarily be easier, but it is perceived to be safer. Change introduces the fear of failure, i.e., one may not be able to make the change desired. If one currently exists at a lower tone, by definition one will have a lower self-esteem, therefore feel guilty about introducing change that is inconsistent with one's own self-evaluation, not to mention alienation from a peer group that may now experience *envy due to one's improvement. Most peer groups will give lip-service approval to step outside the box, as long as you stay inside the circle."*

"The whole thought of moving up in tone may be totally inconsistent with your own self-image, an image that has been created over a lifetime. One has adjusted to a life of failure; therefore, if one's image is altered with an improvement in self-esteem and tone, very likely there will be an increase in expectations placed on you. If success is felt to be undeserved, it will never be thoroughly enjoyed. We see this evidence of disillusionment in people in a variety of circumstances ranging from lottery winners to American Idol winners. Perhaps Austrian psychiatrist Alfred Adler said it best, 'How and to what extent we learn to overcome these feelings of inferiority largely determines our unique personality structure.'"

"Excuse me, Dr. Haviland. I think I'll just tell my friend who couldn't make it tonight he's better off just staying as he is," Gary responded, much to the delight of the class.

"Hold on, hold on. I can't leave you hanging like this, but it is important to note that change is not always easy, and people have a variety of reasons for not engaging in change. Let's treat the topic as if it falls into the good-news, bad-news category, and you have already heard the bad news. Is that okay? What do you think, Gary, would your friend be agreeable?"

"He would be tickled pink," was Gary's response.

"Alright, so let us assume we have completed our self-analysis and identified our shortcomings and come to the conclusion that the benefits derived from the necessary changes are worth the efforts necessary. Can I get an Amen to that?"

"Amen," was heard throughout the class. I walked to the board. *"The first step is to identify which CB's (critical behaviors) are currently being exercised and subsequently affecting one's self-esteem, tone, and inability to experience flow,' not to mention influencing and demonstrating a humorous disposition. This step requires isolation of what you do with your time and in particular your free time."*

The chart has five columns. The first column designates a time period, so I suggest starting at 7:00 p.m. on a Friday evening. For most people, this initiates a period of free choice that spans approximately sixty hours from 7:00 p.m. Friday to 7:00 a.m. Monday. Assuming twenty-one hours for sleep, there are thirty-nine hours that remain.

This division of time reflects the typical nine-to-five forty-hour work week.

Adjust the time sequence on your chart to isolate the approximately fifty free hours that exist outside the work environment, allowing for sleep and mandatory commitments each week. Obviously, this distribution will vary for each person. Label the second column "Activity" and the third column "Critical Behavior." Record the activity that takes place during this time period and then identify each activity as positive (+) if it reflects sharp mental focus, intellect, and your own choice, or negative (-) if it reflects mental drift, emotional influence, or the choice of others. This will require a high degree of self-reflection and honesty to be a valuable tool.

I drew the chart on the board.

Critical Behaviors Activity Sheet

Time	Activity	Critical Behavior (+) or (-)	Tone (+) or (-)	Flow (+) or (-)
Friday 7:00-8:00				
8:00-9:00				
9:00-10:00				
10:00-11:00				
11:00-midnight				

The fourth column is labeled "tone," and the fifth column is labeled "flow." These two columns are subjective in nature; however, they serve to shed light on what is preventing one from being all one can be. Simply reflect on the activity that has taken place during the hour and ask, "Do I truly believe that activity would contribute to raising my tone and moving me closer to the 'Flow' experience? In consideration of tone, simply ask yourself, "Is this the type of activity that one who I aspire to be would engage?" If the response to the tone category is "yes," record a (+); if the response is "no," record a (-). With reference to 'Flow,' ask yourself, "Did the activity serve as a challenge to my existing skills or improve my health?" and record the appropriate response as yes (+) or no (-).

This exercise will allow for a lot of "Gamesmanship" to take place. One may easily justify watching three hours of television as "family bonding" if the children are in the room. I would suggest that an activity that requires an element of interaction with the children may warrant a positive score; however, watching television will be a stretch in most cases. It doesn't mean one can never watch television; just give it the score it deserves.

The tendency will be to assume progress is being made if a number of activities reflect a positive score, and this may be deceiving and serve to keep one constant with where one presently is in reference to self-esteem, tone, flow, and humorous disposition. I would encourage a minimum score of two-thirds of the scoring sheet be positive to indicate growth toward the desired goals.

"So once the self- evaluation and the CB chart have been completed, what's the next step?" asked Mary Ann Jacobs.

"First of all, the CB chart must be completed on several occasions in order to get a comprehensive view of how one's time is really invested. There will be a tendency to use the one weekend of the year when you help fill sand bags for flood victims as indicative of a typical weekend opposed to the three football game weekend," I offered.

"The real progress begins when you reverse the negative critical behaviors that have contributed to getting you where you are today. You may recall the desired state for most people is one of safety and security prompted by emotional responses. Unfortunately, the continued response to emotions leads one to feel out of control, therefore lacking confidence and instilling a feeling of unworthiness."

"The key to tapping back into the mysterious trait known as a humorous disposition is to take risk and accept challenges that will allow your innate sense of spontaneity and curiosity to reignite. The risk can be in any aspect of life. Some

people prefer to start off small by taking a different route to work, stopping at a coffee shop you have never supported, ask a colleague whom you have worked with for years to lunch. The risk activity doesn't have to be dramatic; it simply must be an activity that you have consciously selected. This conscious selection (sharp mental focus) contributes to experiencing the sense of control that serves as the foundation for self-confidence. As confidence grows, one feels competent and worthy to pursue greater challenges. This self-altering sequence continues throughout every aspect of one's life, ranging from what you read, where you go, what you wear, to what you eat, and with whom you associate. Some of the most significant gains in self-confidence will emerge as a result of altering entrenched habits and daily routines, and particularly impactful when applied toward free or leisure time."

The simplicity of this technique is a major hurdle for most people, primarily to those existing lower on the emotional tone scale. Their primary response is frequently, "It can't be that easy!" There is a confluence of negative thinking and experience that supports this line of reasoning, so allow me to identify a few of the more entrenched influences. It may have started early in the developmental years with numerous statements and behaviors articulated within the home contributing to a defeatist nature and perhaps reinforced by a peer group of a similar bent. This is the home environment that early on introduces the expectation of danger, pain, disaster, or the like: terror, dread, and apprehension.

There is a time to be afraid, just as there is a time to rejoice; however, for the individual who exists in this chronic fear tone, his solution to life is to be careful. The thought of change creates great anxiety. Psychologically speaking, the difference between fear and anxiety is that in fear the source of the threat is known, whereas in anxiety it is not.

The late Nathaniel Branden conveys the following insights in his book, *Taking Responsibility:* The more we are aware that we choose our actions, the more likely we are to take responsibility for them. Taking responsibility for our actions is a precondition of taking responsibility for our life. Many adults long to remain children and in fact have never ceased being children. They look to others to tell them what to do. One characteristic of successfully evolved adults is that they learn to take responsibility for their own lives physically, emotionally, intellectually, and spiritually.

The predictable response from one who exists in a fear tone is, "It can't be that easy." Underlying this response is the fear that if they were to try to exercise the discipline necessary to alter behavior, the new solution may not work; then where would they be? Hopefully, they will be able to convince all within earshot, "It can't be that easy," therefore avoiding the need to change or, for that matter, even try.

Individuals of a lower level tone will have no trouble finding excuses or justifications why the critical behavior exercise will not work for them; the real concern is how many others will they convince to remain immobile? Even if people are honest with themselves in admitting or recognizing that their critical behaviors are negative, there will be a lifetime of experience to justify a continuation of the negative behavior. One of the best explanations of the phenomena to continue the negative behavior was offered by Dr. Wayne Dyer in his book, *Your Erroneous Zones*. Dyer exposes the four favorite Neurotic Justifications of the American people: *"That's me," "I can't help it," "I've always been that way,"* and *"It's just my nature."* American people believe just by reciting any one of those phrases (listen closely, at times people will insert all four in one sentence), it rids them of any and all accountability and responsibility to change. Please note, Dyer does label them "neurotic" justifications.

The greater the risk or challenge to the individual, the greater the boost to one's self-esteem. I now refer to this as the "Boyle Effect," named after the unemployed and matronly contestant appearing on the 2009 Britain's *Got Talent* show. She stole the hearts of literally millions of viewers around the world when she sang "I Dreamed a Dream" from the play, *Les Miserables*. This moment captured on tape and played over 300,000,000 times on You Tube is one of the most viewed and certainly one of the more moving events recorded in television history.

The judging panel openly admitted to Boyle, *"When you came out, everyone was laughing at you."* Slight pause, *"No one's laughing at you now.*" The candor and innocence of her response, *"I've never been given the chance before,"* to the panelist pre-performance questioning as to why she has yet to achieve the celebrity artist recognition for which she aspires, is an inspiration to the world. It is one of the most humbling statements I can recall and yet serves to be one of the most motivational I have heard. I am struck by the reality of the number of people who go unrecognized and unnoticed due to "never having the chance." I am also cognizant of the number of opportunities that exist on a daily basis. The difference is Susan Boyle took a risk while millions of others chose to remain safe.

Similar positive reactions have been recorded by viewers of the popular *Dancing With the Stars* television show with respect to the visible change in self-esteem as celebrities in their own right expand in an arena totally foreign to most: ballroom dancing. In their recorded praise of the show, the participants are quick to verbalize how rewarding it is to be challenged in a skill area in which they had not previously been exposed. All-Pro football players subjecting themselves to the ridicule of mass audiences viewing their attempt to perform a rumba or samba have served as an inspiration for literally millions. This is a sample of the *"Flow"* dynamic that was introduced before, stretching an individual in both skill-related abilities and challenge. And more importantly, they are leaving themselves vulnerable to the criticism of others. This is when true growth takes place. The safety net has been removed.

SECTION XI

The Joy of Independent Thought and Choice

"*So Dr. Haviland, what would you suggest I should do in order to experience this awakening?*" Rick Myers asked.

"*I wouldn't make a specific suggestion for what another person might do, for the simple reason what might be perceived as a risk by one individual may not be perceived as a risk by another,*" I responded. "*That's why when you witness someone doing something that you and most people consider risky, you can't automatically give them the benefit and label them as high-tone, self-confident, experiencing 'Flow,' or possessing a humorous disposition. They may not view an activity as being risky because they have developed a skill set which minimizes or eliminates the risk in their view. People who participate in sky-diving and mountain climbing really do not have a death wish, contrary to popular belief. They think that people who drive in rush hour traffic and give public speeches do.*"

I can remember when I gave this presentation to a group of physicians at the home of one of the doctors. He was very skeptical of the theory that risk alone could stimulate one's self-confidence and in turn serve to awaken one's humorous disposition that lies dormant. The host was very insistent that I provide the risk situation for him so that he could experience this growth in self-esteem. The conversation went as follows:

He began, "*So what would you have me do so that I could have this experience?*"

The home audience was very attentive awaiting my response. I gave my explanation about how it was inappropriate for one person to suggest what might be an appropriate risk for another, but he didn't want to hear that, and became more persistent.

"*Go ahead. Give me something. Tell me what to do that will tap into this mysterious trait,*" he insisted.

Given the talk that evening had been well received by those in attendance, I reluctantly made a suggestion in anticipation of moving the program along, "*Okay, Dave, go in the bathroom and shave off your moustache..*"

"*What? You mean to tell me, if I go in and shave my moustache it will enhance my sense of humor?*" He became fully animated as he was dismissing my suggestion.

"That's about the size of it," I insisted.

"Let me be sure I understand this," he continued. *"If I go in that bathroom and shave my moustache, this will in turn affect my self-confidence certainly related to my personality, thus benefitting my patients in a positive manner?"*

"Spoken like a true physician," I said. At this point, physician Dave was grinning from ear to ear, pacing the floor, trying to contain his laughter, fully animated and spirited. I feel safe in saying few of his colleagues in the room had never seen Dave so alive. He was known around the hospital as being rather stoic and restrained. I didn't have to say another word; those present that evening were seeing a transformation that continued to be the talk of the hospital for weeks to come.

Now to the pertinent question, did he shave it?

Not a chance, as I suspected he wouldn't. So much of one's self-image is influenced by our outward appearance and acceptance by others. The mere suggestion of spontaneously changing one's appearance is sufficient to induce a catatonic state for many, including physicians. This is why so many of us continue to wear the same hair styles for decades, drive the same make of car, listen to the same music, continue with the same habits, and the list goes on.

I conveyed the moustache story to the class which generated an energetic exchange led by Rick Myers. *"If that doctor had gone in and shaved his moustache, due to the risk involved, he would have contributed to enhancing his sense of humor, or more technically, his humorous disposition. Is that correct?*

"Spot on," I responded and continued. *"What was being demonstrated and obvious to his audience at his house was that the mere thought of shaving the moustache was tapping into something at a psychological level that was totally invigorating. He was experiencing this spontaneous event at the unconscious level, but the animation in his voice and body were manifested for all to see."*

"What if he had done it?" Mary Ann asked.

"I'm not sure what I would have done, other than to point out that the action was commendable and consistent with accepting the challenge, thus contributing to his self-confidence in the long run. My experience and confidence in the theories

that we have discussed to date in class made me feel I was on pretty safe ground by making the suggestion at his insistence. He wouldn't do it!"

"The risk I took by making the suggestion to the physician was contrary to what I had advised you of before, and that is not to challenge another person because you don't know what they consider risky; therefore, by accepting the challenge, the reality is it may not be risky to them at all. For example, to ask someone to hold a snake would be enough to freak most people out, but to one who was raised near a swampy environment, this may not be a challenging task at all and therefore would have minimal if any impact on their self-esteem. On the other hand, how would they do if asked to give a three minute impromptu speech in front of a class?"

"Don't give my doctor friend undue credit. His profession may influence you to perhaps think that he operates at a different level than others because of what he has accomplished. The truth is the doctor has the same insecurities as the rest of us and operates as the rest of us, and those little black hairs above his lip are as precious to him and his perception of himself. It is very unlikely that he would alter that perception in front of his peers in order to make a point. In some respects, he exists under greater pressure than many community members because he has established himself as a competent individual within the community; therefore, any breach of this may be more detrimental to him. Examples of this extreme pressure are evident when high profile politicians and celebrities, whom society has placed on a pedestal, literally get caught with their pants down. When high profile individuals demonstrate negative CB's, it is difficult for most to comprehend. We expect this behavior from individuals of a lower tone but not from those whom we have elevated in status."

"But Dr. Haviland, don't you think that most people are fearful of this societal judgment coming down on them?" Robin asked.

"Absolutely," was my response. *"And that is precisely why we look to others to tell us what is best for us. Think about it. We select a peer group that is accepting of us; we date people who are acceptable to that peer group; we marry people whom our friends approve of; we take jobs that are respectable to others; we live, dress, and drive what is acceptable to others, and we have children and divorce, if approved by others. And I suspect we will ask for advice from others regarding our funerals. No, wait. Insurance companies already tell us what's*

best for us. So who are we really other than the reflection of whom others want us to be?"

"Think about what we are saying. We live are entire lives from cradle to grave doing what others expect from us in order that we may fit it. And the irony of that is, based on our discussions, if we decide to take charge of our lives by exercising a sharp mental focus, make intelligent decisions instead of emotional ones, and begin to rely on our own judgments rather than the judgments of others...there is a rich, exciting experience that awaits each and every one of us."

"Dr. Haviland, it seems like once it gets rolling on a positive note, everything falls into place.

"Thank you, Mark, but don't be deceived. For everyone who makes it to the sidewalk hall of fame, there is another one who ends up with a tragic story to tell. That's why biographies are so interesting. If you know what you're looking for, it is almost inevitable that you will narrow it down to one individual or one instance when a person allows for mental drift, makes emotional decisions or trusts the judgment of a key person over their own judgment, and the cards begin to fall. This is especially true in the United States, a society where money, greed, and celebrity are valued so highly by so many. And at the same time, there are so many opportunities to drift and make emotionally bad decisions influenced by individuals who don't necessarily have your best interest at heart.

SECTION XII

The Influence of Technology

In recent history, another way of stating, in my lifetime, it was possible to make a mistake in one of the areas mentioned in the preceding pages, but it wasn't necessarily life altering or damaging. In today's technological society, with our handheld ability to capture every conceivable misdeed for perpetuity, it behooves one not to make a mistake. In days of yesteryear, improprieties were very hush-hush and kept within the family. Today, one is fortunate if they can make it to the comfort of their home before the misdeed becomes fodder for anyone who has access to electronic or mobile communication devices. The potential for outside persecution is immediate, unforgiving, and lifelong. Rarely does a week go by when we don't read about an individual taking one's life due to the anticipation of the consequences any one inappropriate action may bring upon that person.

What are the implications of this dynamic as it relates to one's emotional tone or self-esteem? We can already see the influence, as subtle as it may be. We are a society becoming increasingly aware of the exposure and possible ridicule we may receive as a result of any one action that we may commit or opinion we express; therefore, we are withdrawing. We are reluctant to get involved or voice an opinion. Let me clarify that. We are reluctant to get involved when we risk the chance of being identified as a participant. The irony is we frequently want to express an opinion provided we remain anonymous, and many thought that access to the Internet would provide that sanctuary or refuge. Unfortunately, many have learned the hard way that the anticipated anonymity of the Internet is more fantasy than reality.

Recognizing the vulnerability and exposure that comes with involvement, we are increasingly becoming a nation of spectators opposed to a nation of participants. One fourth of prime time television viewing is now comprised of "reality programming." Reality programs could be called "living your life vicariously." How much this transition from being one actively involved in life to one willing to view it only from a distance may be attributed to one's fear of exposure or criticism cannot be determined. The transition has been sluggish in nature but very apparent with each generation.

Within my lifetime, I have witnessed school kids race from school to get on their bikes and pedal to the nearest ball field or engage in make-believe war games as they raced through the woods. Students now wait to be picked up from school, may have a snack when they get home, and then retreat to their room. They emerge from their rooms for dinner that is frequently devoured in front of the television or in competition with social media.

This observation is not to be critical, merely to point out that somewhere along this journey through life, the conclusion was made that it is safer or more rewarding to experience the path traveled by others than to brave our own way. I laughed the first time I saw bowling on television, and I recall making the statement, "Who in the world would sit and watch someone else bowl?" Well, I've learned to keep my mouth shut as I've watch a variety of events generate tremendous viewer support as we tune in to watch others play pool and even cards.

What does it say about our society when *Fifty Shades of Gray* is a bestseller and a record breaking movie at the box office starring two unknown actors? There was a time when the mere suggestion that one would give up participation in a pleasurable activity in order to watch another participate in the same activity was inconceivable.

The introduction of the above topic in the classroom set off a lively debate as a variety of television programming equally divided those who supported a specific program versus critics who couldn't conceive of anyone vicariously enjoying watching someone else play golf, cook, drive a car around a circular track, arrange flowers, or run around an island naked.

"So what's so bad about living this vicarious experience?" Kim inquired.

I offered the following explanation, *"It isn't a question of good or bad. It's the reality that by willingly giving up the experience of participation (living), one is yielding part of oneself to the control of others. In essence, it's the difference between living and taking up space. This lies at the very heart or crossroads of the curiosity and spontaneity of the child yearning to participate by yelling out,*

'Pick me, pick me.' How often have you heard a child yell out, 'Don't pick me. I'd rather watch'?"

Something is happening in our society that is making it more comfortable to participate electronically and anonymously from the comfort of the coffeehouse, camouflaged in passwords and passcodes, than in person. At the same time, there is awareness that the security that has been assumed to be impenetrable is also a myth. While these two remain in conflict, our ability to communicate from one individual to another has been compromised.

"Wow. I think I'm finally catching on," Chrystal Shannon offered. *"It is virtually impossible to choose to be a spectator in life seeking safety and security, avoiding risk and challenge, and at the same time having high self-esteem."*

"Why would anyone choose not to have high self-esteem?" was Robin's question.

Carol responded. *"Can I answer?"*

"Go for it," I urged.

"It's not really a conscious choice. In some respects, early on we have limited control because we are the product of the influences of our home environment and parental influence. The socialization process begins, and we yield to the peer group that is most receptive to us with all the emotional highs and lows that accompany that developmental process," she concluded.

"So it's not my fault I'm so screwed up?" Sam inserted.

My response, *"There is some truth to that. Unfortunately, there does come a point when you must assume responsibility for your actions and become aware that behaviors have consequences. And this is where it gets a bit more complicated because there is no set time or age when this crossroad occurs."*

"If you had to guess, when would you say it occurs?" Reid asked.

"Again, impossible to pin it down due to the diverse backgrounds we represent; however, we certainly can identify some stages that one would suspect would be critical in forcing these choices that are so instrumental in our development," I offered.

"Like when?" Jason prompted.

I responded, *"In addition to the home environment experienced in our youth, I would suggest the selection and activities of a specific peer group would be huge in influencing one's ultimate disposition. In the old days it was the smokers versus the non-smokers, the jocks versus the hoods, the band members versus the drama club, and the list goes on. The point being, during those formative years, it is difficult for one to be proactive and maintain a sharp mental focus. The truth of the matter is we are adrift, and the primary influence on which way we go is frequently determined by which group is the most accepting of us."*

Parental influence also becomes a major player during these formative years. This is obvious with examples like regulating study time and curfews, especially once driving privileges are granted. Bear in mind, some individuals never do assume responsibility for their actions, and I think we have all witnessed this. It is easy to envision for many students who attend college apart from what they do with their free time, true independence and decision making may be postponed until graduation."

"But eventually we are faced with the big three CB's, is that correct?" Marti quizzed.

"Precisely," I concurred.

"Would you say one's 'emotional tone' is established before or after the CB's come into play?" Jennifer asked.

"I think it's safe to say the emotional tone is established rather early, primarily due to the parental influence in the home environment. We pick up their cues as to whether or not this world is a safe, adventurous place to live or if every situation holds an element of danger. However, as much as we would like to lay the blame at the feet of our parents, we eventually are responsible for the decisions we make, which in turn influence our movement on the tone scale," I summarized.

"The good news is, regardless of the past influences, we modify and mold what currently is by the decisions we make in the next year, month, week, day, and hour. We become the architects of our future; that's why I like that CB exercise. We identify what behaviors are taking us where we want to go and continue to reinforce them while eliminating those actions which are counterproductive to where we want to go and who we want to be." I was enthused.

Glenn Wright contributed, *"And if I understand this in its entirety, it is essential that one have high self-esteem and exist high on the emotional tone scale in order to experience 'Flow' and possess the humorous disposition essential to lead."*

"Accurate, to the letter," I responded. *"Class dismissed."*

SECTION XIII

Epilogue

How do you find your niche in life? Identify the pain and suggest the cure.
-Unleash Your Greatness (Olson & Strand)

The first edition of this book did not have an epilogue. I felt that I had adequately conveyed the techniques necessary for an individual to "Bridge the Communication Gap" in order to successfully engage, and reap the benefits thereof. At the time it was written, approximately six years ago, that was true. In some respects, I flattered myself and anticipated it would fill a void that had existed since Dale Carneigie's bestseller written eighty-four years ago. What I didn't account for was the change in society that took place as we transitioned from a society of "poor-communication" to one of "no-communication".

I will leave it to the historians to determine if this breakdown in communication was necessary or inevitable. Regardless, it affected an entire generation. As most would agree, we are a product of our times. Therefore, we witnessed the demise of civil discourse throughout society. It first became apparent on college campuses. If speakers with opposing opinions were invited, they were quickly dismissed by angry voices and protest that made civil discourse virtually impossible. Eventually, many speakers abandoned that effort for fear of their own personal safety.

Another popular technique was to shout down, or talk over any dissenting opinion, resulting in total withdrawal from any dissension. We chose to ignore each other. To suggest that this technique of withdrawal causes a problem for successful engagement is the epitome of an understatement. So how does this societal phenomenon of withdrawal affect the implementation of some of the techniques outlined in this book?

The essential drivers of engagement; recognition, trust, coaching and the conveyance of care for an employee are mute. It becomes extremely difficult to maintain a humorous disposition in a vacuum which occurs within an atmosphere of hostility. It becomes ludicrous to seek to raise emotional tone in a combative stagnant climate. The mood that exist once withdrawal or cancellation of another's opinion becomes the predominant model, is the antithesis of the state of consciousness required to achieve "FLOW." If there is a winner in this depressed atmosphere of restricted response, it may be the academicians. Now they have no one to challenge their views.

The dilemma is the average adult has become a master of delusion and deception (DD's), and isn't aware of it. We don't necessary lie to one another, we just suppress the truth in this "no-communication" world in which we live. The saddest part is, it is virtually impossible to identify this state of delirium due to the fact that we surround ourselves with people and media who all drink from the same cup of delirium. Therapist have now assigned labels to it and recognize the symptoms of 'cognitive dissonance' and 'confirmation bias.' That only compounds the problem. It now makes it easier to talk about these lost souls.

This dichotomy reminds me of two previous careers in my past. I had the opportunity to buy a health spa when I was in Australia teaching. This teaching appointment of two years, (passage and taxes paid), was my first job immediately following graduation from the University of Miami. I was flattered by this appointment when I was informed that I was selected from thousands of applicants. I later realized it was due to the fact that I had already fulfilled my military obligation (USMC), by service in Vietnam, that made me such a desirable applicant for Australian residency. My apologizes to those thousands, especially those with high draft numbers at the time.

My initial intention was to make the spa very exclusive and private, selling memberships to close jock friends, rugby and cricket players, and generate just enough revenue to keep the lights on and the water hot. However, that was not to be. Former members were knocking on the door hence it was open to the public. During the membership application process as personal goals were established, I was amazed with how out of touch people were with themselves. Very few identified themselves as obese or overweight. The reason for that is they could always identify someone much larger and "they certainly didn't have that problem". I see a parallel to this in contemporary society as it relates to communication. The popular technique is known as deflection. If one begins to feel defensive about a particular position or belief they have taken, they can always cite an offender of greater stature than themselves guilty of the same. This deflection negates any further criticism of them or the position they have taken.

The second insight I have gained, in addition to adults' willingness to play verbal volleyball adnauseam, was gained while working with convicted felons. Some were incarcerated and others were threatened with incarceration if they didn't abide by the rehabilitation program outlined for them. First, there was usually a precipitating event that contributed to the behavior, and second, it was seldom that I ran across a truly remorseful convicted felon. I met many who would verbalize remorse, especially in front of the parole board, but for the most part the only thing they truly regretted was getting caught. This observation applied to simple larceny from a building (shoplifting) to murder.

From a research perspective, I have always been fascinated by what makes individuals successful. This explains my patronage of Carnegie not only in his ability to isolate specific techniques for success, but to identify isolated events that contributed to both the success or demise of an individual.

Perhaps this interest is what contributed to my curiosity regarding convicted felons. Obviously, these are individuals who have committed offences toward individuals or society. It is easy to identify a pattern of crime once one commits to the lifestyle. However, it is possible to isolate a specific precipitating event that caused commitment to the initial offense and subsequently, the lifestyle. In some cases, that precipitating event may amount to the day one decides to run with a different group. Why? Because of loneliness or because of their willingness to accept you as you are?

I took personal satisfaction in uncovering the precipitating event during an intake investigation. For example, I interviewed a middle-aged man living quite comfortably with his wife, and he was now picked up for larceny from a building for stealing a can of Sure deodorant. At the time of apprehension, he had sixty-seven dollars in his pocket and absolutely no justification for his actions. He reviewed his suburban lifestyle, praised his grandchildren etc. but was clueless regarding his behavior of that afternoon. He admitted, he was mildly upset with his wife who that morning insisted they were going to the lake cottage. He had no desire to go. He sought refuge temporarily when he went to the mall where the offense took place. He also offered, "And I don't even use Sure deodorant." However, his wife did. The precipitating event.

A man convicted of murdering a woman who had car problems and approached him as he was locking up his service station for the evening was critical of her for being out so late. Not for a minute did he contemplate perhaps his actions were inappropriate. In the book, *Living, Loving, & Learning*, Leo Buscaglia quotes Nikos Kazantzakis, "You have your brush, you have your colors, you paint paradise, then in you go." Buscaglia goes on to say, "And if you want to paint hell, go ahead and paint it, but then don't blame me, and don't blame your parents and don't blame society...and for goodness sake don't blame God. You take full responsibility for creating your own hell. So much beauty is lost because we are afraid."

I learned early in my criminal justice career, aside from personal freedom the most desirable provision for an inmate: silence. It is amazing how the level of communication, and quality of information is enhanced if one is able to reserve a quiet conference room away from the cellblock in order to conduct an interview. The constant droning of victimization, and the continuous clanging of cell doors becomes deafening over time.

I use these examples to illustrate a point. As adults, it is very difficult for one to recognize and admit fault and inappropriate behavior. As adults, we become masters of defensive posturing making it very difficult to hold us accountable. In summary, the techniques outlined in this book work and have stood the test of time. The techniques are as relevant as they were in Carnegie's day eighty-four years ago. The problem is the audience has changed and now reflects a culture of narcissistic heightened individualism and self-obsession that has tremendous difficulty accepting responsibility for behavior.

Another incident which I considered to be a form of self-love while I conducted an intake interview with a young man accused of larceny in a building which is classified as a felony. His scam was to steal the student backpacks that were placed in open wooden cubicles in the bookstore at Western Michigan University. This drop off was required by the bookstore as the students shopped.

Pawning these items was proving to be a very lucrative occupation for this young man. When I attempted to guilt-trip him by asking, "How would you feel if someone did that to you?" His response, "I would have no problem with that." He went on to explain, "Anything that is left unattended is open game." This included items in your backyard, garage and picnic basket. I struggled with this interpretation until I heard it a year later from my employer and headmaster at the school where I taught in Australia. It was the same premise, and he had a name for justifying the action. He called it, "The Law of Allurement." I guess it's all a matter of interpretation, as is the example below.

I recently heard a speech presented by an activist to a high school audience. The speaker encouraged the chant of, "I am somebody, respect me, protect me, never neglect me." I realize the intensions were well meaning. However, if the message is interpreted to mean these qualities can be granted or bestowed on one, by another, it is terribly misleading. Those desired outcomes cannot be demanded and can only come from within the individual. They must ensue as a result of a life reflective of positive critical behaviors.

I have certainly heard my share of hard luck stories over a lifetime. I could catalogue a listing of victimization statements as to who's fault it really is that you are in the predicament that currently exists. I was sympathetic to many of these excuses until I came across a particularly moving testimony when I was in Paris, France presenting a workshop.

The story is of Dominque Bauby, editor of the French Elle magazine. In 1995 he suffered a massive stroke paralyzing his entire body from his head down. His brain function remained intact. His body was immobilized with the exception of his ability to blink his left eye. This is referred to as "locked-in syndrome." One of the conference attendees gave me the book, The Diving Bell and the

Butterfly that describes Bauby's ordeal. The miracle of the story is that Bauby wrote the book **<u>after</u>** he suffered the stroke, blinking one letter at a time. This was possible by a carousel that was constructed to rotate the letters of the alphabet around the ceiling of his hospital room.

If your hard luck, poor-me story exceeds Bauby's I am all ears. If not, let's pick up the pieces and get on with living the life that awaits. There are too many exceptions to the rule of people who have overcome tremendous odds and have created exemplary lives to jump into a pity-party now.

"Life isn't about finding yourself. Life is about creating yourself."
-George Bernard Shaw

SECTION XIV

'On My Way Project'

Given the current generation is having a great deal of difficulty stepping up to the plate and accepting any degree of responsibility for their behavior, I would like to look to the future, and focus on the youth of today.

Is there light at the end of the tunnel? Yes, there is and it is found in Section VII in the discussion involving self-esteem. Section VII outlines the development of self-esteem. We know that attitudes and behaviors are a reflection of one's self-esteem. We know self-esteem is a reflection of those critical choices or behaviors one makes along the way. It must ensue.

By way of review, life is a series or sequence of events and opportunities. These moments are continuous throughout a lifetime. These moments arise, and we make a choice, or choices, by combining the three behavioral options:

1) Maintain a Sharp Mental Focus or Drift;
2) Exercise Intellect or Emotions;
3) Utilize Your Own Judgement or The Judgement of Others.

For self-esteem to be enhanced one must choose the critical behaviors (CB's), that evolves from a sharp mental focus, is intelligent in its origin, and sponsored by the individual who will be affected. Behaviors that result from mental drift are emotional in their makeup and are influenced by others and may be detrimental to the enhancement of self-esteem.

Obviously, there are numerous daily decisions that don't carry the weight of the world as a result of the action taken. Whether or not one eats a banana or an orange may not be impactful. However, a daily selection of a piece of fruit or a jelly-filled donut may have consequences over time. This is where the element of common sense plays a part. Unfortunately, that particular sense is not as common as one would hope.

Some people refer to these decisive moments as precipitating events, i.e. what happened or what thought process took place prior to your action? Note, the precipitating event may be positive or negative.

Your reaction is what is critical. Successful people can list an entire sequence of events that were instrumental in their success and they write about that in their autobiographies. Self-esteem is acquired due to action and behaviors, not bestowed or given by someone else. Follow behaviors, they become the blueprints for self-esteem.

As previously suggested, unsuccessful people will also provide an ample list. This will be a listing of victimizing people and statements that are responsible for their failures. And they may be very articulate in stating them. They have rehearsed these explanations for years. In some respects, this represents the state of drift mentioned previously. 'Drifting' is a negative state of mind conspicuous by its emptiness of purpose.

The **'ON MY WAY'** project' will address the development and enhancement of high or positive self-esteem directly. It is my intention to have the youth of today fully realize they are the architects of their own destiny. This destiny is built on the decisions and behaviors they manifest on a daily. These decisions become the building blocks of positive self-esteem. Self-esteem is an individual's subjective evaluation of their own worth. If and to the extent that one lacks self-esteem, they feel driven to fake it, commonly referred to as pseudo self- esteem. The reality is, control your own destiny or someone else will.

ENGAGEMENT...for an eight-year-old would begin with a thorough explanation of terms and definitions relating to self-esteem and the role it plays in development and achievement of goals in life. This will be facilitated by flash cards and class discussion. A mini-journal to record self-esteem efforts will be distributed and a board game that demonstrates progress will be introduced. The teacher maintains custodial privilege over all efforts. Periodically, the child will transfer the journal listings and board-game progress to an autobiographical, hard covered book entitled, "On My Way." This book is also available on disk and is a keepsake, complete with pictures if desired, and the sole property of the student.

The hard copy may be printed at the suggested conclusion date (twelve-years of age), or any time during the self-esteem exercise. The entire project continues as the student matriculates to the next grade level. The concepts underlying positive self-esteem will be well established at this time. It is anticipated that many students will continue with journal and/or disk entries for years to come.

Learning Styles...are primarily visual, auditory and kinesthetic. The 'On My Way 'project incorporates all three learning styles therefore catering to the desired learning style of the individual.

ASSESSMENT

WHAT IF…the concept of self-esteem is introduced at a very early age? Perhaps the age of eight years. This suggested age would allow a certain degree of common sense and judgement to be present, as well as verbal skills, and hopefully, prior to a variety of negative influences. For those skeptics who insist it is already too late, I would suggest an ambitious plan of corrective action utilizing the formula above. These turn-around efforts can be very rewarding to the parties involved. Most significantly, youth have not refined their level of justification, denial or rebuttal that the parents have.

IMAGINE IF YOU WILL…an entire family that engaged periodically in this review of selected behaviors. Now I don't live in a cloud I realize that train of intact families has left the station. It is nice to dream. This is why I feel this effort must be handled within the school system, preferably at the third-grade level.

CONCEIVE OF A SCHOOL SYSTEM…comprised of a student body that is well versed in discussions relating to incidents that required a sharp mental focus, intellect or personal judgement.

CONSIDER…an entire school system and community that is well versed in the efforts necessary to achieve positive self-esteem and achieve personal and professional goals.

WHO BENEFITS…in addition to the individual? Each family member related and associated with an individual with high self-esteem benefits from their example. Every mental health agency in the community that deals with anxiety, depression, suicide, alcohol and drug abuse, and domestic abuse benefits from a population of high self-esteem individuals. Every agency affiliated with the criminal justice system benefits from a population of high self-esteemed individuals due to a decrease in populations representing probationers, paroles, and incarcerated individuals. Health providers are free to focus on individuals with serious health problems opposed to patients experiencing health problems that are self-imposed by definition. School administrators and counselors are free to focus on educational needs.

APPENDIX A

'On My Way'

The 'On My Way' project is a companion to the *book; Bridging the Communication Gap* by author James Haviland. The intent of the project is to present the materials in Sections VI and VII in the book in a manner catering to a more youthful audience. Both sections deal with the origins and maintenance of self-esteem. This project will require a more interactive engagement than that of the adult reader. The focus is for an audience of eight to twelve- years, or third to sixth grade.

The major premise of the project is to enhance and create an awareness of one's 'self-esteem' by recognizing their role in elevating the same. Self-esteem is a subjective evaluation or opinion of ones' own worth. Self-esteem is the opinion one has of oneself. There is no value-judgement more important to an individual than the estimate they pass on themselves. This determination is made by the individual and subsequently influences their behavior. The purpose of this project is for an individual to record specific behaviors enacted that will enhance their own self-esteem and encourage them 'On Their Way' to becoming the successful person they desire to be.

The project requires a notebook for journal entries, a Building Bridges Board (3- B) with stickers, and eventually an avenue to publish the beginning chapters of an autobiography. The autobiography will be a hardbound book reflecting life experiences to accompany the early critical behaviors that contribute to a positive self-esteem. This book may be published at the end of the third grade of school or postponed until the completion of a school project that will continue through sixth grade.

The project board has a unisex silhouette in the middle with the caption 'On My Way'. Radiating out from the silhouette are eight avenues of exit, each having a cobble stone bridge midway. The bridge provides an opportunity to lay thirty to fifty paving stones. The eight exits are located on the four corners of the board and midway on each side. The exits are labeled; Friendships, Hobbies, Acts of Kindness, *Occupation, Volunteer Work, Savings, Fitness & Health and Education.

*Occupation may refer to current efforts reflected by allowance, paper routes etc. It may also reflect time invested in researching possible careers that are of interest. This may be an expressed interest in becoming a professional athlete, airline pilot, attorney etc. or interviewing the same to gain insight to the profession.

The journals are identified by the 'On My Way' silhouette sticker provided and self-applied. The journal is also divided by the student into eight sections corresponding with the eight exits on the Building Bridges Board. Stickers identifying the eight exits are also provided. Each entry in the section shall begin with the date and a listing of the self-esteem activity that took place. The student then transfers one cobble stone sticker to the bridge that corresponds with the appropriate exit. This represents visual confirmation of their efforts to become the person they want to be.

Once this has been completed a check mark is placed next to the journal entry to indicate the cobble stone has been placed on the board. At the end of the school year or periodically during the school year, the student records the efforts they have put forth to reach their individual goals by making a computer entry to their autobiography. This entry is produced in hardback copy at the time of their choosing. Ideally this will be at the end of the four- year project. This visual documentation instills in them personal pride, elevates self-esteem and provides concrete evidence to them that they are 'On Their

Way' to becoming the person they want to be. Realizing you are the architect of your own destiny, what a precious keepsake.

"Life isn't about finding yourself. Life is about creating yourself."
-George Bernard Shaw

Appendix B

'On My Way Tutorial'

*This entire session between the tutor (T) and the student (S) may be taped for prosperity. Director (D).

T: Do you know what self-esteem is?

S: No.

T: Do you know what an opinion is?

S: The way you think? D: Coach them to accepting this definition via numerous examples. T: Let's do some examples. What is your favorite sports team, television program, subject, color etc.

T: Why do you like that particular one? S: Explains.

T: Is that every ones' favorite? S: No.

T: What you have said about your favorite may or may not be true, but it is what you believe to be true? S: Yes. T: This is what an opinion is. Your best guess as to what is true.

T: Let's go back to the word esteem. Esteem simply means highly or favorable opinion. So, what would the word self-esteem mean?

S: It would be my opinion of myself. T: BINGO!

T: So, let me ask? What is your self-esteem, or opinion of yourself and why? D: In the event the responses start to be negative, redirect them to the fact 'esteem' is favorable. D: You may wish to write their responses down briefly.

T: If you wanted to raise your self-esteem or your opinion of yourself what would you have to do?

S: I would have to do good or positive things.

T: Could you give me some examples of what you might do? D: Let them go and try to remember those that directly relate to the Building Bridges Board; Friendships, Hobbies, Acts of Kindness, Occupation*, Volunteer Work, Savings, Fitness & Health, and Education. D: See prompt questions APPENDIX C.

*Occupation may relate to current responsibilities like paper routes, raking leaves or chores granting allowance. It may also reflect time spent researching occupations to which they have expressed an interest. Interviews of individuals currently or previously employed in that occupation may also be considered.

'On My Way Project'

Stage Two

Once the student is clear regarding the definition and how one raises self-esteem (positive behaviors that enhance one's opinion of self), introduce the option of recording by date, the actual behavior that takes place. This will require a journal that has been divided into the eight categories represented on the Building Bridges Board.

At the appropriate time, the journal entry will be transferred (via sticker or coloring) to the Building Bridges Board for a visual representation of progress. At this step in the process, it may serve as a time to share experiences that have taken place within the desired areas of development.

Midway or at the conclusion of the school year the students will reflect on their progress that has occurred and blend these positive results with other events that have taken place like a summer family trip etc. These biographical events will be published in a computerized hard cover book entitled 'On My Way'. Each student will have their own hard-covered book, and if desired by the student the publishing may be postponed until the same process is repeated the following year(s). The end result will be a critical awareness on the part of the child during their formative years of the role they play in developing their self-esteem and becoming the type of person they desire to be.

"Life isn't about finding yourself. Life is about creating yourself."
-George Bernard Shaw

APPENDIX C

Prompts for Building Bridges Board Categories

Friendships

1. New Students
2. Neighbors
3. Correspondence

Hobbies

4. Pets
5. Activities
6. Lessons

Acts of Kindness

7. Helping Others
8. Visiting Seniors
9. Animal Support

Occupation

10. Current Responsibilities (allowance related)
11. Researching Future Opportunities
12. Interviewing Previously Employed

Volunteer Work

13. With Elderly
14. Outside of Home
15. With Families in Need

Savings

16. From Current Allowance
17. Gifts Received
18. Bank Savings Account

Fitness & Health

19. Current Exercise Program
20. Eating Habits
21. Organized Activity

Education

22. Attendance
23. Outside of School Educational Programs
24. Lessons of Instruction/Information

SECTION XV

Resources

Resources

Ailes, Roger, with Jon Kraushar. *You Are The Message: Secrets of the Master Communicators.* Homewood, Illinois: Dow Jones-Irwin, 1988.

Barreca, Regina. *They Used to Call Me Snow White...but I Drifted.* New York: Penguin Books, 1991.

Bauby, Jean-Dominique. *The Diving Bell and the Butterfly: A Memoir of Life Death.* New York: Vintage Press, 1997.

Bellah, Robert. *Habits of the Heart.* Berkeley: University of California Press, 1985.

Bennett, William J. *The Book of Virtues.* New York: Simon and Schuster, 1993.

Bennis, Warren. *Why Leaders Can't Lead.* San Francisco: Jossey-Bass, 1990.

Bloom, Allan. *The Closing of the American Mind.* New York: Simon and Schuster, 1987.

Branden, Nathaniel. *The Psychology of Self-Esteem: 1969, Breaking Free:1970. The Disowned Self:1972,* Los Angeles: Nash Publishing Corporation. *The Power of Self-Esteem.* New York: Barnes & Noble, 2001.

Buscaglia, Leo. *Living, Loving & Learning.* New York: Holt, Rinehart and Winston, 1982.

Canfield, Jack. *The Success Principles.* New York: Harper Collins Publishers, 2005.

Clark, Karen Kaiser. Life Is Change *Growth Is Optional.* St. Paul Minnesota:

Csikszentmihalyi, Mihaly. *Good Business.* New York: Penguin Group, 2003.

Csikszentmihalyi, Mihaly. *FLOW: The Psychology of Optimal Experience.* New York: Harper & Row, Publishers, 1990.

DePree, Max. *Leadership Is An Art.* New York: Doubleday, 1989

Dyer, Wayne. *Your Erroneous Zones.* New York: Avon Books, 1976.

Eadie, Betty. *Embraced By The Light*

Freud, Sigmund. *Jokes and Their Relations to the Unconscious.* New York: Norton, 1960.

Funk, Wilfred. *Word Origins and Their Romantic Stories.*

Gardner, Gerald. *All The Presidents' Wits:The Power of Presidential Hum. 1986.*

Gerzon, Mark. *Choice of Heroes: The Changing Face of American Manhood.* Houghton Mifflin Company, 1992.

Goleman, Daniel. *Working with Emotional Intelligence.* New York: Bantam Books, 1998.

Hill, Napoleon. *Law of Success.* Chicago: Success Unlimited, Inc., MCMLXXIX.

Hill, Napoleon. *Outwitting the Devil: The Secret to Freedom and Success.* New York: Sterling Publishing Co., Inc. 2011.

Himmelfarb, Gertrude. *On Looking Into the Abyss:Untimely Thoughts on Culture and Society.*

Hunter, James C., *The Servant:A Simple Story About the True Essence of Leadershp.* Roseville, CA: Prima Publishing, 1998.

Iacocca, L. *and* Novak, W., *Iacocca: An Autobiography.* New York: Bantam Books, 1984.

Karsan, Rudy and Kruse, Kevin. **WE**: *How To Increase Performance and Profits Through Full Engagement.* Hoboken, New Jersey, John Wiley & Sons Inc, 2011.

Klein, Allen. *The Healing Power of Humor.* New York: G.P. Putnam's Sons, 1989.

Kruse, Kevin. *Employee Engagement 2.0.* Richboro, PA: The Kruse Group, 2012.

Langelett, George, *How Do I Keep My Employees Motivated? The Practice of Empathy-Based Management.* Austin, TX: River Grove Books, 2014.

Leider, Richard. and Shapiro, David. *Repacking Your Bags: Lighten Your Load for the Rest of Your Life.* Berrett-Koehler Publishers, Incorporated, 1995.

Lencioni, Patrick. *The Five Dysfunctions of a Team.* Jossey-Bass, San Francisco, CA. 2002.

Lester, Julius. *"Whatever Happened to the Civil Rights Movement?"* as cited in Sykes, Charles A. *A Nation of Victims: The Decay of the American Character.* New York: St. Martin's Press, 1992.

Maltz, Maxwell. *Psycho-Cybernetics (updated Edition).* Fine Communications, 2002.

Marsh, Abigail. *The Fear Factor: How One Emotion Connects Altruists, Psychopaths, & Everyone In-Between.* New York: Hachette Book Group, 2017.

Maslow, Abraham H. *"The Jonah Complex",* as cited in *Interpersonal Dynamics.* Homewood, Illinois: The Dorsey Press, 1968.

Maslow, Abraham H., *Motivation and Personality, Harper & Row, New York, 1954*

McGhee, Paul. *Humor:Its Origin and Development.* San Francisco: W.H. Freeman and Company, 1979.

Mindess, Harvey. *Laughter and Liberation.* Los Angeles, California: Nash Publishing, 1971.

Minshull, Ruth. *How To Choose Your People.* Scientology. Ann Arbor, MI 1972.

Naisbitt, John. *Megatrends.* New York: Warner Books, 1982.

Peele, Stanton. *The Diseasing of America.* San Francisco: Lexington Books, 1995.

Olson, Rick J. and Strand, Robert. *Unleash Your Greatness: Become a Person of Impact.* Richmond, Virginia, 2002.

Redfield, James. *The Celestine Prophecy.* New York: Warner Books, 1993.

Schieffer, B. and Gates, G.P. *The Acting President: Ronald Reagan & the Supporting Players Who Helped Him Create the Illusion That Held America Spellbound.* 1990.

Smiles, Samuel. *SELF-HELP.* London: John Murray, 1859.

Storr, Will. Selfie: How we Became So Self-Obsessed and What It's Doing to Us. New York: The Overlook Press, Peter Mayer Publishers, Inc. 2018.

Sykes, Charles J. *A Nation of Victims.* New York: St. Martin's Press, 1992.

Tannen, Deborah. *You Just Don't Understand.* New York: Ballentine Books, 1990.

Tenge, Jean M. and Campbell, W. Keith. *The Narcissism Epidemic.* New York: Simon & Schuster, 2009.

Trueblood, Eldon. *The Humor of Christ. 1975.*

Ventura, Jesse. *I Ain't Got Time to Bleed: Reworking the Body Politic from the Bottom Up.*

Wyden, Peter. *The Unknown Iacocca. 1987.*

Zunin, Natalie. *Contact:The First Four Minutes.* New York: Ballantine Books, 1972.

Zweig, David. *Invisibles; The Power of Anonymous Work in an age of Relentless Self-Promotion.* Penguin Group (USA) LLC. New York. 2014